INVESTIGATING ROBBERY

Investigating Robbery

MICHAEL BANTON
Professor of Sociology
University of Bristol

Gower

Published by
Gower Publishing Company Limited,
Gower House, Croft Road, Aldershot, Hampshire, England.

Gower Publishing Company,
Old Post Road, Brookfield, Vermont 05036, USA.

ISBN   0 566 05114 1   1494216

Printed in Great Britain by
Paradigm Print, Gateshead, Tyne & Wear.

Contents

List of tables

Acknowledgements

This study was possible only because a number of busy detective officers gave of their time to advise on the best way of carrying it out and to help in assembling the necessary information. Peter Beardon, Larry Bill, Roger Grimshaw, Geoff Roost and Don Taylor were particularly helpful. (I do not list their ranks in the hope that were I do so this information would soon be out of date.) However the Avon and Somerset Constabulary accepts no responsibility for the veracity of the descriptions of cases. These are presented in a manner which should make it impossible for anyone who was not a party to one of them to discover from this study the identity of any victim, suspect or witness. If these persons were referred to by pseudonymous family names there would still be the possibility that the name used might seem to identify someone living in the locality. Therefore members of the public have been described by a first name other than their own, plus an initial.

Most university research in the social sciences needs the support of a grant from an outside body to meet the extra expenses entailed. This study was an exception. I should, however, express my appreciation of the contribution of Mrs. Jacqueline Bee in typing the report in addition to all the many other duties she carries out for our department.

Michael Banton.

Department of Sociology
University of Bristol
January, 1985

1 Introduction

Early in 1978 the Royal Commission on Criminal Procedure was appointed to review the powers and duties of the police in respect of the investigation of offences, and the arrangements for the custody and prosecution of suspects. I was a member of this Commission. After it had reported, three years later, I was asked by the Assistant Chief Constable (Crime) of Avon and Somerset Constabulary, whether the Commission had considered examining in detail the adequacy of police powers for investigating particular kinds of serious crime. I was able to tell him that the Commission had indeed considered this as a possible approach (at my own suggestion, as it happens) but had decided against it. Looking back, I thought they had been right to do so since the necessary research would have had to stretch over too long a period of time. Nevertheless I did still believe that this might prove a rewarding approach.

After a further year had passed I returned to this matter, telling the Chief Constable that I thought my university timetable would allow me to study a sample of cases of serious crime and analyze the investigational problems they presented. In my own mind I thought it might be best to concentrate upon the receiving or handling of stolen property, or perhaps burglary, but the Chief Constable, after discussing the possibilities, said he thought it would be best if I were to look at offences of robbery since these were about the right number (303 in 1982) for me to be able to study all the cases for one year, and they were concentrated in a particular part of Bristol which would make it easier for me to maintain contact with the detectives investigating them. So I agreed to examine the robbery cases for 1983.

The Theft Act of 1968 says that a person is guilty of robbery if he steals, and immediately before or at the time of doing so, and in order to do so, he uses force on any person or puts or seeks to put any person in fear of being there and then subjected to force. A charge of robbery is a serious matter that can be tried only on indictment, that is, before a judge and jury in the Crown Court. It is the kind of crime that arouses the fear of members of the public, and it has been increasing over the years. The police figures for robbery in Bristol over a period of 44 years are set out in table 1.

Table 1
Robbery in Bristol, 1939-83

Year	Total Crime	Cases Detected
1939	6	1
1959	15	10
1979	82	19
1983	148	41

According to the 1981 British Crime Survey (Hough and Mayhew 1983, p.9), the official statistics seriously under-record the true incidence of robbery. In this survey, 11,000 people were asked about their experiences during the previous twelve months. According to their replies, on 47 per cent of the occasions that people experienced robbery or attempted robbery a report was made to the police, yet in only about 11 per cent of cases can this have resulted in a record in the official statistics. This discrepancy may stem from several sources: members of the public may exaggerate their experience of robbery, or their reporting of it, while the police may not always accept that the alleged incident constituted a robbery. With a sample of 11,000 the number of robberies alleged was small, making any generalizations suspect, though it did suggest that there were twice as many victims under the age of 45 as over, and twice as many men as women. Many of the alleged offences that were not recorded may have been minor occurrences. According to another section of the same survey, 28 per cent of people living in inner cities believed robbery to be very common; 72 per cent of the same people singled out this offence as having become more common during the past 5 years (Maxfield 1984, correction slip). Twelve per cent of inner city residents said they never went out at night because

2

they were afraid for their personal safety. The survey was repeated in 1983. Preliminary figures indicated that in the two-year period there had been a 9 per cent increase in the experience of robbery and that 73 per cent of such cases involved sums of less than £25.

Table 2
Robbery in England and Wales, 1939-83

	Total Crime	Cases Detected
1939	227	96
1959	1,900	906
1979	12,482	3,882
1983	22,100	5,300

Note: The figures for 1939 represent the annual average for 1935-39. The figures for robberies detected in 1939 and 1959 are the number of persons 'for trial', whereas those for 1979 and 1983 are of cases 'cleared up'. Over the period 1970-83 the clear-up rate for robbery in England and Wales altogether has declined steadily from 42 to 24 per cent.

Over the period 1975-84 the number of recorded robberies in Bristol varied between 119 (47 detected) and a high of 313 (106 detected). In so far as there is a generally rising trend, the 1983 total represents a decline, falling back to a figure below that recorded for 1977. (It rose to 271 in 1984.) Robberies are committed much more frequently in particular localities. Avon and Somerset has a total area of 480,000 hectares, or 1,700 square miles, and a population of 1,370,000 people. Of 250 robberies in 1983, 206 were committed in Bristol; 148 of these were in A division, covering the centre of the city, and 109 of the offences occurred in the sub-division covered by Trinity Road Police Station. This includes the 'red light' area called St. Pauls and it is widely known as the locality in which there was a serious riot in April 1981. Many black people, and particularly unemployed young black males, live in this area.

From the beginning it was my belief that the growth in the number of robbery offences was to be explained by an increased belief among young men that they could 'get away' with crimes of this kind; that they could commit them without being recognized and without afterwards feeling guilty about what they had done. If a few could obtain an extra income in this way, apparently with impunity, others would copy them and would take their standards from them. It was not the kind of offence to be expected in a neighbourhood in which the residents were well known to one another and the informal

3

social controls were strong. Nor was it the kind of offence for which offenders would travel appreciable distances to get away from their home territory. Since the police cannot be everywhere (and who would want them to be?) and since robbery is often committed in places where the offence cannot be observed by witnesses, no increase in the number of police officers on patrol, I thought, would reduce the incidence very much. Nor did I believe that any increase in police powers, e.g. to detain or question suspects, would make much difference. The source of the problem lay in the social life of the neighbourhood and its relation to the wider society. Nevertheless, I thought that a detailed examination of cases might correct or help elaborate these presuppositions.

Since the detectives at this station had a lot of work to get through, the best way of carrying out the research would have been for a full-time research worker to accompany the detectives in the course of their investigations. This method has been employed (e.g. Steer 1980), but I did not have more than one day a week available. The plan therefore was for me to visit the sub-division each week, hear about any new cases, and inform myself concerning the progress of investigations into earlier cases. The police put aside for me photocopies of the 'crime form' made out when the offence was reported, and of any statement taken from the aggrieved person. In consultation with the divisional Detective Superintendant and the sub-divisional Detective Inspector, it was decided that the investigator should submit forms A and, if applicable, B (see appendix) recording the number of hours expended by detectives and uniformed officers in various phases of the enquiry. This would provide a measure of the resources devoted to the investigations. The inspector would also complete an assessment of the original report allocating points to show the priority he thought it deserved in comparison with other crime reports which made calls upon police resources (form C). This process is called screening. It has been used as a means of managing investigations in some police departments in the United States but its use arouses hot debate in Britain. Some police officers take the view that all reports must be investigated as thoroughly as possible because the police owe that duty to the aggrieved. Others reply that it is often apparent at the outset that a report is unreliable or provides too little useful information to hold out any hope of success, and that to pursue such matters is to take resources away from investigations that could lead to detections.

The expectation that I might spend one day a week at the station or with the detectives was not realized. The detectives assigned to robbery investigations were not necessarily working on them at the times I was available; there were weeks when, because of the pressure of work arising from a major incident, it was not convenient for me to visit; and there were weeks when, because of other commitments, I could not get to the station. There were, of course, all the minor difficulties because particular detectives were working other hours, were on leave, sick, or away on other duties. So I became dependent upon the assistance of a few supervisors and detectives who took messages as necessary and watched over the preparation of the forms. Any other than observational research with the police seems always to involve the filling of forms but there is now so much paper work in policing anyhow that police officers are in general ready to help in this way when they believe the research to be worthwhile.

The number of cases which I followed is slightly greater than the number officially recorded. Whenever an initial report was classified as a robbery or an attempted robbery by the officer who received it, I included it in my figures. Further investigation of some cases led the police to the conclusion that no offence had actually taken place and these were recorded as 'no crime' and taken out of the official figures. In some other instances what initially appeared to be a robbery was officially recorded as some other kind of offence, usually as theft and once as 'demanding money with menaces'; these were not counted as robberies because the element of assault on the victim seemed to be only technical. Whereas the official figures for A division of Bristol record 148 robberies (including attempted robberies) I have worked with a total of 157.

Robbery offences are so much more frequent in one particular locality because the city's prostitution is concentrated there and many of those robbed are either the clients of prostitutes or men who have come there look for them. It is also includes the sorts of housing to which alcoholics and social incompetents gravitate, and they are often the victims of robbery. These characteristics are reflected in the breakdown of the cases which I use for the next three chapters. Chapter Two examines the 108 'street' robberies (of which 15 were detected); Chapter Three the 23 robberies that occurred in shops, housing, banks or other enclosed premises (of which 15 were detected); Chapter Four covers the remaining 26 cases (12 detected) which were directly associated with prostitution, drugs and drunkenness. Two robberies that occurred in taxis have been included with these remaining cases.

There is a contrast between the everyday reality of crime as it is known to police officers, solicitors and magistrates, and the image of crime as it is fashioned in the mass media and in some sociological writing. Most crimes are far too trivial to be mentioned in the press, but to understand them as incidents it is necessary to know about the parties, their history, relationships, and their mental states, in the detail that is reserved for the spectacular crimes that, from time to time, are discussed at very great length. Most robberies are trivial events; that is why few of the alleged occurrences are reported to the police and why many that were recorded in Bristol in 1983 are described here only in outline. Yet it is necessary to provide some account of them if the reader is to appreciate the diversity of the incidents that make up this total in the criminal statistics. This account may also provide some corrective to the over-simplified images with which the press necessarily operates, and to the commentaries which insinuate that concern over the rising number of robberies is cultivated in order to sell newspapers. These case studies combine with the findings of the British Crime Survey to show that robbery and the fear of robbery greatly reduce the quality of life for everyone who lives in or uses the neighbourhoods where it has become prevalent.

2 Street robberies

The street robberies can be divided into five categories. A significant proportion of cases are started by men who make false reports to cover their own behaviour. They have spent their money on prostitution, gambling or drinking and feel they should account for having lost it. So they come to the police and allege that they have been robbed. It is well, therefore, to distinguish between those cases in which there is independent evidence that a robbery occurred, and those which depend upon the testimony of the aggrieved party alone. Table 3 shows how these cases are distributed.

Table 3
Street Robberies, by sex of victim and evidence

	Male	Female
Independent evidence	13	8
No independent evidence	64	7

Where a man and a woman were together, this has been counted as the robbery of a man. Independent evidence is most frequently provided by the testimony of other witnesses of the offence, but it may also be of a physical character, as when

7

someone reports that a social security book has been taken and that book is afterwards found on waste ground and handed in to the police.

Table 3 does not include an important category of street robberies which need separate consideration. These are robberies of people who are known to be carrying cash or valuables that can easily be resold. Such people are the men who come round the houses collecting the money from the gas and electricity meters, collecting rents, subscriptions to clothing clubs and charitable bodies, and door-to-door salesmen. Of these, 13 were male and 2 female.

This chapter will first present the general charcteristics of the 108 reports of street robberies and then take up specimen cases of the various sub-categories to consider the problems they posed to the investigators.

Table 4
Street Robberies, by the time of offence

Time	Cases
0000–0159	11
0200–0359	15
0400–0559	5
0600–0759	0
0800–0959	1
1000–1159	5
1200–1359	4
1400–1559	8
1600–1759	10
1800–1959	13
2000–2159	15
2200–2359	21

It will be seen from Table 4 that most robberies occur during the hours of darkness, though a significant number occur in daylight. Few of the female victims were robbed between 2000 and 0600, doubtless because not many women are to be seen unescorted on the streets in this locality at that time; nearly twice as many of the men were robbed between 2000 and 0600 as during the day.

Table 5
Street Robberies, by reporting intervals

Reported	Cases
within 30 minutes	58
30 minutes to 1 hour 59 minutes	23
2 to 11 hours	10
12 to 24 hours	7
over 24 hours	7
Information missing	3

Note: in three instances the time of the alleged robbery could not be established.

Table 6
Street Robberies, by alleged loss

Value of goods or money	Cases
Zero (includes attempted robbery)	19
less than £10	11
£10 - £99	54
£100 - £499	16
£500 - £999	4
£1,000 and over	4

Table 7
Street Robberies, by age of victim

Age	Cases
Less than 18 years	12
18 - 29 years	30
30 - 59 years	49
60 years and over	8
Information missing	9

The analyses presented in Table 5-7 did not uncover any important associations between times, reporting interval, loss or age, on the one hand, and the availability of independent evidence or the sex of the victim. However, and not surprisingly, where the victim was a known carrier of cash the case was more likely to be given a high score when screened by the Detective Inspector (Table 8). Reports of robbery in which there was no independent evidence as to the offence were allocated less time in investigation than others (Table 9). Over half of the unsupported allegations were given less than 5 hours.

Table 8
Street Robberies, by scores when screened

Scores	Cases	Detected
0 – 3	25	0
4 – 6	27	1
7 – 9	32	5
10 – 12	7	2
13 – 15	9	4
16 – 18	5	2
19 and over	3	1

Table 9
Street Robberies, by hours in investigation

Hours expended	Cases	Detected
0 – 5	48	1
6 – 10	26	3
11 – 19	20	4
20 – 49	10	5
50 and over	4	2

Table 10
Street Robberies, by outcome

Detected as robbery	10
Detected as theft	5
Reclassified but not detected	1
Recorded as 'no crime'	3
Suspect identified but insufficient evidence	5
Dubious report	22
Report filed	62

In virtually all the cases in which the report was filed this was because there was so little information that could lead to the identification of the offender that it was not worthwhile spending more time on enquiries, though when offenders were taken into custody for similar offences they would be questioned about these ones to see if they knew anything about them.

STREET ROBBERIES OF MALES, INDEPENDENT EVIDENCE AVAILABLE

Of the 13 cases in this category, 3 resulted in prosecutions. In the first cases police actions are described in some detail to indicate the general practice. In subsequent cases these descriptions are briefer.

123.   Victor W. was walking in the City Centre at 0040 when he was set upon by another man who stole his jacket.   Uniformed officers spent 6 hours with the complainant, 3 hours on house to house enquiries, while 2 hours were given to scene of crime examination.   Detective officers spent 8 hours with the complainant, 5 hours on house to house enquiries and 1 hour touring the area with the complainant and a friend of his.   A further one hour was spent by the detectives at the scene.   The friend had witnessed the attack and he identified Charles S., age 19, as the attacker.   Charles had the stolen jacket with him;   he was taken into custody and charged. Two hours were spent on his arrest, 2 on interviewing him, 1 on investigating his background, and 8 on preparing case papers for court.   On committal to the Crown Court he pleaded guilty and was sentenced to perform 200 hours community service.

140.   Albert C., age 12, was walking with a friend when a man demanded money from him with a threat of violence.   The boy took the robber to his home where, subject to further threats, he produced £10.   He provided a good description of the robber.   Uniformed officers spent 3 hours with the complainant.   Officers of the Street Offences Squad spent a further 2 hours with him, 2 hours touring the area with him, and 1 hour showing him photographs of possible suspects to see if he could make an identification.   The robber had said he would call upon the victim the next weekend.   When he arrived the police were waiting for him.   He was David W., 16 years, described as a student with an address in Sneyd Park.   He was charged with robbery and blackmail.   At the Juvenile Court he was also dealt with for theft and criminal damage, being made subject to a supervision order for 2 years and ordered to pay £150 towards the cost of the prosecution.

79.   Samson A., 33 years, a student, was friendly with a fellow Nigerian, Simon O.   Simon had a dispute with his wife, who packed her bag and went to the address of her sister Mary N. where she met Samson. Then Simon appeared, in a state of distress, accompanied by two police officers.   He accused Samson of being involved in his wife's departure. Mrs. O. left with the police officers.   Samson left and shortly afterwards withdrew money from the bank to pay his rent.   He drove off

with £300 in his shirt pocket. Shortly afterwards his car was stopped by Simon, armed with a chain and a knife, who threatened his life. Simon caught his arm with the chain, grabbed the ignition key, and allegedly pulled the £300 from his pocket. A house to house enquiry located witnesses to a struggle between the men but there was no evidence that the money passed into Simon's possession. The detective said 'it's like a domestic dispute less £300. It's a shame that it has to be a robbery charge but as there was no injury it is difficult to see what other charge would better fit the circumstances'. After a committal to the Crown Court, Simon was found not guilty of robbery.

In four other cases enquiries came to nothing or resulted in conviction for another offence.

82. Barry C., a 7 year old boy, was en route to the shop to buy cigarettes for his father when he was stopped by four girls of about 14 years who demanded his money and eventually forced the £2 from his fingers. The boy called his dad who gave chase, but was stopped when one of the girls smashed a bottle and threatened him with it. (The detective wondered why a grown man had been unable to deal with a schoolgirl?) Enquiries were made at the school. When interviewed one girl admitted to having been present but named the friend of hers who had been responsible. This was checked with the victim. It was then discovered that the suspect had returned to Jamaica so the report was filed.

91. Richard H., 28 years, while walking past the Black and White cafe at 0325 was stopped by 3 young males and 1 female; they demanded money, knocking Richard to the ground and robbing him of £53. The victim was shown photographs of possible suspects and identified a woman who had seemed to be with the group though she was not one of his attackers. She had earlier been involved in prostitution in Bristol. Later she was arrested in Birmingham and brought to Bristol; no useful information could be obtained from her and she had an alibi placing her in Birmingham at the time of the robbery. So the charge against her was refused. Bristol officers spent a total of $5\frac{1}{2}$ hours on the initial investigation and 11 hours dealing with the suspect. For lack of additional evidence the report was then filed.

122.   Colin C., 64 years, a resident at the nearby reception centre, was walking along Ashley Road at 2030 when he was set upon by three men who took from him £30, his pension book, army discharge papers, etc. As they held him face down he could provide little identification.   The following day Bernard C., 58 years, of no fixed address, tried to withdraw money from the local post office using the pension book. The name and address on it had been altered.   Bernard admitted receiving the book knowing it to have been stolen but little useful information could be obtained from him.   Bernard was prosecuted at the Magistrates' Court for handling stolen property and for forgery; whilst on bail he absconded, being finally convicted at Crown Court where he was sentenced to 18 months imprisonment (9 months of which were suspended). There being no other leads as to the original report, it was filed.

14.   Herbert T., 40 years, was in the car park at Lawrence Hill Health Centre at 2130 hours when he was approached by two young men who demanded money and, when refused it, attacked him with a sharp instrument causing a stab wound to the left side of his abdomen. £30 was stolen from him.   At 2202 the victim entered the police station in a state of near collapse. Within 7 minutes an ambulance and nurse were in attendance.   The victim had undergone serious abdominal surgery within the previous year so the police were concerned about his condition.   At 2215 police officers left to search the scene and to secure the victim's car.   A dog handler and dog followed.   A police officer was sent to make enquiries at two clubs which the victim might have visited or intended to visit.   A police sergeant went to see the victim's wife.   At 2312 a detective phoned from the hospital; he had been able to obtain a little extra information from the victim that might lead to an identification. At 0053 a witness to the robbery was located. Uniformed officers spent 19 hours and detectives 26 hours on these enquiries.   It was regarded as a priority investigation, scored 20 by the Detective Inspector, but there were few leads to follow.   Other robbery suspects in custody were later questioned about it.   The victim's description of his attacker matched that of Donald R., arrested subsequently for cases 10 and 15 which are discussed in Chapter Three. When Donald was put on an identity parade in connection with these cases Herbert attended.   He said that his attacker was either Donald or another man but

then settled for the other.   Donald would not admit to being involved in this offence.

The remaining cases may be summarised more briefly.

1.   Andrew S., 26 years, knocked unconscious to the ground while crossing College Green at 0100.

29.   Brian D., 62 years, returning home at 0330, was set upon by 4 or 5 youths who demanded money.   One of them stabbed him in the hand, resulting in his being detained in hospital for two nights, but they got nothing from him.   One suspect was interviewed and 16 hours were spent on interviewing him but no one could be charged.

35 & 36.   Cuthbert P., a young man, and his girl friend were together threatened by 5 youths in Ashley Road at 0230 and £3.50 taken from them.

54.   Paul A., 29 years, driving with a friend, was involved in a very minor road accident at 2145. Possibly as a result, they were surrounded by a group of youths.   Paul was punched and £37 taken from his pockets.

60.   Cecil W., 16 years, in City Road at 0225, was threatened with a screwdriver by a youth who took from him a brown leather flying jacket valued at £140.

63.   James W., and Peter D., both 18 years, at 0220 in Park Street, were robbed of £15 by a group of some 8 young men. At the time they were very drunk.

Whenever it seemed worthwhile, police officers took the aggrieved individuals on a tour of the area to see if they could identify suspects.   They often re-interviewed them a little later to see if they had recollected anything else that could be of help but frequently they had too little information to provide any adequate lead.

STREET ROBBERIES OF MALES, NO INDEPENDENT EVIDENCE AVAILABLE

Of the 64 cases in this category, 5 resulted in prosecution and conviction for robbery. They were

18.   Philip W., aged 25, had been in a club which was frequented by male homosexuals.   At 0230, outside the

club, he was assaulted and sustained minor injuries. A gold chain worth £100 and a wallet with £14 were taken from him. The man who was with Philip was assaulted and hospitalized. He would not talk to the police when visited in hospital. Philip reported the offence two hours after it occurred; the day following he withdrew his report, but the police were dissatisfied since they believed his original account to be truthful. They re-interviewed him without result. The police continued to question suspects in custody matching the description and two months later Alan Y., while arrested for case no 41, admitted to this robbery. It was taken into consideration when he was sentenced for the more serious offence.

68. Stanley M., was in Park Street at 0230 when a man grabbed him from behind and demanded his wallet. Two police officers on plain clothes patrol in an unmarked police car at the time were informed. They saw 3 men fifty yards away who fitted the description and arrested them on suspicion of robbery. Uniformed officers spent 2 hours on the arrest. CID officers spent 8 hours interviewing them, 2 hours investigating their background, and 16 hours preparing case papers. The trial took another 16 hours. At it Percy S., was charged with assault with intent to rob and fined £50.

77. Roderick M., 18 years, was in Braggs Lane at 2215 when someone demanded with threats, a medallion and chain he had round his neck. Uniformed officers spent half an hour at the scene and half an hour touring the area with the complainant. A police constable went to the local park and found there a youth answering to the description who was wearing the medallion. Two hours were spent with the complainant, including the taking of a statement. Detectives spent an hour on similar matters and 3 hours preparing case papers. At his trial, Robin G., 17 years, was also convicted of unlawful and malicious wounding of another man and sentenced to 9 months youth custody.

121. Stephen P., 60 years, in central Bristol at 2230 one Friday night was knocked to the ground, threatened with a knife and robbed of £35. The police officer who received the aggrieved's report noted that he was quite intoxicated; details as to the location of the alleged offence and descriptions of the two men said to be involved were difficult to obtain, so the allegation might be false. There were no leads at all

15

for the detectives to follow.

At midday on the Sunday, the body of William B. was discovered in a house by one of the two lodgers, Maurice A. and Ronald P. They were both arrested on suspicion of complicity in homicide. As they did not appear to be obvious suspects, enquiries started into their associates. It was learned that Ronald had earlier in the year, shared an address with, inter alia, Thomas J. and Milton H. Thomas had recently been committed for trial on a charge of murdering a woman at her home address. Milton had previous convictions for burglary, theft, and violence; recently he had been found tampering with motor cars near public toilets frequented by homosexuals, and when approached, had produced a knife. His description had recently been circulated as he was wanted in connection with enquiries into theft. Arrangements were made to try to arrest Milton on the Tuesday.

On the Monday a man told police about a barwoman who had spoken of a man called Milt in whom the police should be interested. The description fitted Milton. The witness said that Milt carried a knife. Later that evening he returned with the barwoman who said she had been out for a drink with Milt the previous Thursday, and on the Friday met him again together with a friend of his called Andrew D. Milton and Andrew came to her pub on the Friday evening. They were short of money. Milton said they would go out and get some. Shortly afterwards they returned and, when asked, Milton said he had obtained money by robbing someone at knifepoint. She doubted if he was telling the truth. On Saturday lunchtime Milton and Andrew came to the pub; after closing time the three went for a walk. In the course of this Milton pointed to a place where he said he had carried out the robbery (it was the same place as that reported by Stephen).

That evening, while she was working behind the bar, the two appeared again, short of money, and rather drunken. They went out, Milton stating that there were going for more money. After about an hour they returned with money to spend. Milton asked her to go out with him for a meal and, when she declined, became angry. He took out his knife and said 'Do you realize I've killed a man tonight?' She thought it was the drink in him that was talking. The two left. Later the barwoman went home and did not return until the

16

Monday when she learned for the first time of the murder and spoke with the man who had told the police of her suspicions. The barwoman was able to tell the police about Andrew's address.

Her information indicated that Milton was a dangerous character so his arrest had to be planned with care. After arrest Milton and Andrew both admitted to the robbery of Stephen and to having gone to burgle William's flat. When he realized that William was inside, Andrew had run off. Milton entered alone and acted alone in killing William. He said he could not remember doing it. He only remembered finding himself covered in blood.

The barwoman sought to protect Andrew and would not mention him at first since she believed him to be a nice lad being dragged down by Milton. She was difficult to interview. Because of the urgency of the case and the need for the information to be shared by a small team, at least 6 officers (including a Detective Superintendant and a Detective Inspector) worked a stretch of over 24 hours duty, 4 of them for 31 hours. The arrests involved upwards of 30 officers; one incident room was reponsible for the submission of all relevant statements and follow-up enquiries. In these circumstances it is impossible to calculate separately the time spent in the investigation of the robbery.

146. Francis B., 38 years, at 0010, was stopped and assaulted by three youths who took £100 from him. Uniformed officers spent an hour touring the area and looking for possible witnesses. Detectives spent nearly four hours with the complainant, on house to house enquiries, and in speaking with witnesses. No leads could be found. As a result of an anonymous telephone call naming them, two suspects were arrested; 14 hours were spent questioning them, 20 hours on background investigations and 10 hours preparing case papers for court. The two charged were Burton D., 20 years, a parolee, who justified the attack by saying 'he had a knife' and Alec S., 20 years. Since the accused first assaulted the victim and then subsequently formed an intention to steal, they were charged with assault occasioning grievous bodily harm and with theft. Burton was sentenced to 2 years 3 months youth custody and Alec to 15 months youth custody.

In six cases the detectives had a lead which came to nothing or the original report was reclassified.

28. Roger W., 53 years, in Grosvenor Road at 1740 was approached by 3 youths who demanded money from him. When they found he had none they went off. The police showed him photographs of possible suspects. He identified one. This man was arrested on suspicion and interviewed (taking up 12 hours of police time). He refused to answer some pointed questions about his movements at the time in question. The aggrieved said he would neither identify his assailants nor would he give evidence in court. The arrested man was then released as 'refused charge' (i.e. the supervisory officer refused to charge him as the evidence was insufficient). Another suspect in custody was questioned about the same incident without result. The report was then filed.

56. Alan H., 18 years, reported that about 3 months previously a youth named as Karl S. had demanded money, telling him to get some or he would regret it. He gave him £10, £4, £5, £20, £6, on various occasions. The police spent 2½ hours with the complainant and witnesses, 2 hours arresting and interviewing the offender, and 2 hours preparing case papers. He was prosecuted as a juvenile for three offences of blackmail being fined £50 on each, ordered to pay £35 compensation and £35 costs.

61. Rodrigo D., 16 years, at 1245 in the central city had his wages packet snatched by two youths. He could provide only a very poor description of them. As he had sustained no injuries this was reclassified as theft and filed.

70. Norman F., 17 years, at 0215, was set upon by one of a group of youths, his watch ripped off, a ring taken from his hand and money from his pockets. He was then approached by another group of youths one of whom took a jacket from the victim who was hit on the head. Two cars containing youths arrived; the man who had taken the jacket went off in one of them. Police officers investigating a complaint from Norman later identified this car and found that the jacket had been left in it. Uniformed officers spent 3 hours with the complainant, half an hour touring the area with him, 1 hour at the hospital and six hours with witnesses. Detectives spent a total of 17½ hours on similar enquiries, including checking with dealers who might

18

have been sold the stolen property. Five youths were arrested on suspicion, after some had been identified by the victim as members of the second group; 11½ hours were spent with them. One of these youths was a juvenile, Joseph M., who had apparently taken Norman's coat. He denied having been in the area at the time, let alone having been involved in any incident. He was released into the custody of his father. Later he was reinterviewed in the presence of the mother of one of his friends. When the aggrieved saw Joseph he did not identify him as a participant in the robbery, so Joseph was charged with theft. He admitted this offence and was later fined £50 with £20 costs; the original robbery remained undetected.

86. Ibrahim H., 11 years, was playing in the park when he was grabbed by another boy who took his watch. The police spent 2 hours with the complainant, including a tour of the area with him to see if he could spot the culprit. Detectives spent two hours talking with people round about, and, having obtained a lead, 2 hours on enquiries with another police force. A neighbour suggested that the offender might be Gordon H. He was arrested, interviewed without positive result, and released.

152. Albert S., 24 years, was outside the Black and White cafe at 1530 when five youths surrounded him; one held a knife against his stomach and demanded the stereo recorder which he was wearing. They took it, and £5, and warned him not to go to the police. Uniformed officers spent 2 hours with him, including the showing of photographs, and detectives 1½ hours. A suspect was identified, arrested, investigated, and interviewed (taking a further 6 detective hours). He did not fit the description well enough and was later released.

In five cases the allegation was withdrawn, or the report marked 'no crime'. They were:

4. Charles R., 29 years, said that at 2135 he was walking along a footpath when 3 youths robbed him of £40. The police doubted the story, since no robbery had ever previously been reported in that locality and the description of his attackers was so poor. He was brought back to the station the following day when he retracted his allegation. He had probably been drinking or gambling and wanted to account for no longer having the money. The case took 2 hours of

19

police time.

13A.   Morris B., 28 years, was a representative for Bristol Rovers Lottery Club.   He had been out drinking with his brother and reported that at 2230 when passing through a pedestrian subway he was accosted by 5 youths who robbed him of £69 and a number of lottery tickets.   The police showed him photographs.   They tried to contact his brother.   They learned that Morris himself subsequently returned the missing tickets to the club.   He was asked to return to the police station where, under questioning, he admitted that his original report and signed statement were false.   He was then charged with theft.   After conviction he was fined £100.   The police spent 6 hours on the original report, then 4½ hours on the investigation of the alleged theft.

25 and 31 both relate to Cyril T., 41 years, a man who lives in Bath but comes regularly to St. Pauls to play darts in a pub.   He was introduced to customers there last year by a West Indian called Dave.   One Sunday he was asked to drive two black darts players home to Easton.   He first reported that while in the car he was asked for £10 and that later his wallet was snatched.   He implicated Dave.   A week later he wrote a letter in which he said 'I have made a tererbel mistake in saying it was Dave . . . he is one of the best friends, Black friends I have . . .'.   On the same day he reported a second robbery.   He said he was sitting in his car when two men held a penknife to his throat and demanded money.   He gave them £28 and they ran off.   The police spent 4½ hours on his case. After receiving the letter they reclassified the first report as 'no crime' and they remained sceptical about whether the second had occurred.   The aggrieved did not appear to be a reliable witness.

102.   Peter G., 17 years, was walking through an underpass when he was set upon; two youths held him down while another two went through his pockets and took £18.   The officer who took his statement was not persuaded by it so he checked the records using the Police National Computer, learning that earlier in the year the aggrieved had been officially cautioned for wasting police time.   The scene of the alleged incident was searched without any evidence being found.   The complainant was reinterviewed the following day by a detective who thought him of low intelligence.   He made a new statement, retracting the

previous one, and declaring 'The reason why I made the story was because I lost £15 of my wages . . . I couldn't pay the rent and I owed them £15. I just thought to try and get an excuse for delaying the repayment'. This was therefore recorded as 'no crime'. It was not thought worthwhile to prosecute him for an offence. The matter had taken 3 hours of police time. A slightly unusual feature was that in the first statement he described his alleged assailants as all being of Asian appearance.

In 13 other cases there were grounds for doubting the veracity of the original report. On average, four hours of police time was given to their investigation.

6. Josiah P., 52 years, was stopped in the street at 2215 by a youth who asked him for money and hit him; he was then hit by another youth but nothing was taken from him. The aggrieved would not talk with the detective investigating the complaint. Shortly afterwards he was admitted to a psychiatric hospital but after discharge was still unwilling to talk further.

16. Duncan H., 62 years, when returning from a public house at 2300 was allegedly stopped by a man who grabbed his tie, pulled it tight around his neck and robbed him of £30. When shown photographs he made an identification, but the man so identified had an alibi for the time in question. The aggrieved then went to Cheltenham where he was involved in a fight and was taken into intensive care at the hospital. Afterwards he disappeared and could not be reinterviewed.

17. Harbinder S., 58 years, was stopped in a pedestrian underpass by a man who tried to take £5 from him. The aggrieved, who had been drinking, said at the time that he was threatened by two white men; at another time by one coloured man. He was shown photographs, though the police doubted whether there had been any attempted robbery.

47. John W., at 0300 was approached by some men who took £15 from him. He reported this to the police two days later because he had applied to the DHSS for benefit and found that they will not listen to stories of loss by crime unless the alleged offence has been reported to the police. He told the police he had not reported it earlier because he felt soft. House to house enquiries were negative.

51.   Derek W., 27 years, said that at 0930 in a quiet lane three men robbed him of £32.   Though he said he was in conversation when these men grabbed him he could produce no witness and reported the incident only after 3 days so that he could claim from the DHSS.   The aggrieved lived 5 doors away from the complainant in case no. 47 and the allegation was made just two weeks after his, so there might be a connection.

52.   Geoffrey W, 32 years, asked a youth for directions at 0030 and then was chased by this youth and 6 others who robbed him of £40.   The area was toured with the complainant and house to house enquiries were made but no witness could be found.   It proved impossible to contact the complainant to reinterview him and the detective was not convinced of the truth of the story he had told.

76.   Stanley R., 49 years, a fisherman from Lowestoft, said he was attacked by three men at 2300 hours, wounded, and robbed of £46.   The address he gave in Lowestoft proved to be false and the jacket he alleged stolen was not found.

84.   Hugh M., 30 years, at 0230 was knocked to the ground by two men and his wallet with £50 was stolen. After reinterview the detective reported that the aggrieved was quite drunk at the time; that he accepted that instead of £50 he could not have had more than £6–7 left at the time in question; that the descriptions given at the second interview differed greatly from the those given at the first; that the complainant was on bail on an assault charge and might be trying to confuse that issue; that the defendant denied that he had imagined the robbery, but that his denial was neither as firm nor as indignant as might be expected.

85.   John G., 51 years, alleged that outside the Black and White cafe he was robbed of £5 and his DHSS claims book.   The aggrieved is too severely addicted to alcohol for any reliance to be placed upon what he says.

95.   Raymond J., 13 years, alleged that at 1115 one morning he had his athletic shoes taken from him under threat of assault by another boy; the latter said that he would get them back if he stole a pair of 'trainers' for him.   He told this story only after he

had been arrested for stealing these 'trainers' from a shop. The complainant refused to contact the detective to try to establish the identity of the boy who had taken his shoes, and, after talking with his mother, the detective suspected that it was a false allegation intended to cover his own guilt to the theft charge. As no progress could be made with the robbery report it was filed.

96.   Gerald B., 20 years, alleged that he was robbed in the street of £40 DHSS money by 2 youths. A police sergeant reported 'Unfortunately for Gerald at the time he was being 'robbed' his double was seen by a P.C. on foot patrol sitting in the Daily Diner. Gerald had a number of cuts and abrasions on his hands and forearms which he says he sustained earlier in a dispute with his wife. She no doubt relieved him of his money as well'. It was noted that 'he did not waste much time in claiming a refund from the DHSS'.

128.   Anton P., 24 years, an Italian tourist, said that at 2320 hours while in the street, he was grabbed from behind; then someone appeared in front of him, punched him in the stomach and took his body belt containing £3,000 worth of American Express travellers cheques. Enquiries at the scene found no witnesses. Nor could the complainant be reinterviewed. Enquiries at the address he gave first brought denials that he lived there and then that he had stayed there for one day before moving to London without leaving any forwarding address. American Express had not been notified of any loss and could provide no details of missing cheques. The police doubted the extent of the loss. They suspected that the complainant had been with a prostitute and had then been robbed of a lesser amount.

131.   Nigel F., 21 years, a visitor from Gloucester, said that in the street at 0040 he had been attacked by two men who took £101 from him. He made the report to the police in Gloucester who questioned the story because of his inability to provide any description of his alleged assailants. Again, he may have been robbed, but the sum alleged stolen may have been inflated.

There remain 36 cases of street robberies of males in which there is no independent evidence but no reason to doubt the veracity of the reports. These cases attracted, on average, a priority screening score of 6 from the Detective Inspector

23

(not a high average) and on average 8½ hours of police time was devoted to their investigation.

9. Keith M., 25 years, was stopped at 2045 by a man who threatened him with an iron bar, demanding money. The aggrieved escaped, called 999 within 2 minutes, and provided a description of his assailant. The police toured the area with him, and showed him photographs, but without result.

26. William R., 57 years, in a pedestrian underpass at 1815, was robbed of £15 by 3 youths. Not reported until the following day because the complainant is of a nervous disposition and does not want to have police officers calling at his home.

27. Royston H., 39 years, while on his way home at 1820 was robbed of £20 by 3 youths – probably the same three responsible for the previous offence.

38. Nigel M., 21 years, a visitor to Bristol using an underpass at 2100, was robbed of £17.50 at knife point by 3 youths. Since the complainant left the city it was difficult to follow up the report.

39. Maurice C., 34 years, is known to the police as a white homosexual who lives with his mother in the heart of St. Pauls. At 2345 one evening he went out to buy cigarettes, and was approached by a man who asked him the time and a further series of questions, ending with a demand for money. Feeling threatened, the complainant handed over £5. The man said £2 would be enough as he only wanted to get some fish and chips. The complainant said that the £5 was all that he had. The man was then seen getting into a car, the registration number of which was, taken by the complainant. The car was seen empty later and observation maintained. A man called Walter, known to the police, came up to it. He denied having recently driven away a man who had been engaged in such an offence. The complainant did not recognise Walter, so he was released and the enquiry came to a dead end.

46. Raymond J., 21 years, at 1555, while in a big block of flats, was grabbed by 2 youths who held a knife to his stomach and took £25 from him.

50A. Lawrence M., 18 years, in the street at 0535 was confronted by 4 youths who attempted to take the gold rings from his fingers and when he turned to run away he was struck in the back by a knife. Lawrence had been at a party in the vicinity where these rings had probably been noticed. The two young men who were with him at the time were both known to the police and one of them was suspected of having been involved in the robberies on Ali (no 19) and Mohammed (no 40). The offence was reclassified as assault occasioning grievious bodily harm. Those responsible for it appear to have been from London, being associated with a disco group but not personally known to the group's organizers. They could not be identified.

55. Oswald K., 69 years, was in the street at 1040 when two young men pushed him to the ground and searched his pockets. When their victim shouted, they ran off. A local P.C. suggested two possible suspects; they were interviewed without result.

58. Kenneth W., 24 years, at 1140 was held up at knife point by 3 youths who took £15 from him. He could provide only very poor descriptions of these youths.

59. Michael K., 53 years, at 2335, was searched at knife–point by 3 youths. A tour of the area with him proved negative and he was shown photographs of possible suspects without result. (It will be noted that there was a sequence of reports referring to 3 youths. Community constables and patrol officers were asked to look out for youths answering the description who went around in groups of three.)

62. Harbinder S., 58 years, is the same complainant as in case no 17. On this occasion he alleged that while crossing a footbridge over the motorway, he was assaulted by two youths and robbed of £84. A witness confirmed that she had paid him £93 shortly before. Another witness heard him call for help, and 'stop thief!' at the relevant time. This witness had come across and had chased two black youths who were running off. The complainant first said that he had been robbed by two black youths but he appeared very drunk; taken on a tour of the area he identified numerous people, black and white, male and female, as responsible. Later he made a statement describing his attacker as a single white male.

64. James H., 11 years, at 1715, was robbed of his wristwatch by another boy. The offender could not be traced.

78.　Eric S., 32 years, said that at 0100 he was looking for a bed and breakfast place. Passing the Black and White cafe he enquired of some youths but they accused him of being a police informer. About 10 of them attacked him taking £90 and his watch. He could not describe any of them. The reason he gave for being in this area at the time was not persuasive; the detective thought that he could have been with a prostitute and wanted a story to cover the loss of his money.

88.　Keith E., 34 years, at 0105 had two men grab him and steal his wallet with £2.50; he suffered a slight injury.

89.　Philip D., 37 years, at 2100 while drunk, had £340 taken from him by a group of 8-10 youths. He could recall nothing about his attackers.

93.　Maurice C., 34 years, was the victim of an earlier robbery (no 39) nearly six months previously. He was persuaded (by someone described by a detective as a strong minded woman) to burgle the flat of a next-door neighbour who was in hospital. He stole £5,000 and, with his share, went into the local pub, spending freely. Later he was robbed of property worth £120. The detective said that he is epileptic, alcoholic, homosexual, now mentally disturbed and 'God knows what will happen to his poor old mother when he is sent to prison'. Maurice claimed to have discovered the burglary but there were discrepancies between the accounts he gave to the police and to the neighbour's relatives which caused his guilt to be discovered. After conviction he was sentenced to 18 months imprisonment suspended for two years and made subject to a Supervision Order for 12 months, so he did not go to prison after all. The alleged robbery of him remains undetected.

98.　Eleven days later the same man was the victim of an attempted robbery by 3 youths. (In the following year he was robbed once again leading the police to describe him as being almost a professional victim).

107.　Paul W., 26 years, at 0145 in the street, was robbed of £8.50 by 3 youths.

108.　Alex P., 44 years, at 0250 was surrounded by five youths and something held to his throat while £87 was taken from him. The detective described the complainant's statement as 'worthless'. He was known to have stopped his car outside the Black and White cafe and to have asked where he could get a girl. He was told to drive round the corner and wait. Scenes of crime officers examined the car, found one impression on the roof but could make no identification. Some of the complainant's papers were later recovered from an adjacent road.

109.   Jeffery D., 31 years, left the Black and White cafe in the early hours and at 0430 in a nearby street was pushed into a garden by 2 youths who stole £110 from him.

112.   Donald F., 43 years, at 2200 was grabbed by 3 youths who robbed him of £60. Invited to tour the area with the police, he declined. On reinterview he was unable to add anything to his original account, which offered very little go on.

113.   Alistair H., 32 years, reported that at 2130 he was driving along the main road from the M32 to the city centre on the way from his home in the Cotswolds to visit his parents-in-law's house in one of the most respectable neighbourhoods in Bristol. According to a statement he made to a P.C. at 0010, a man got out of the driver's seat of a car at the side of the road and flagged him down; when he stopped he was attacked at knife point by three black youths and robbed of cash and property to a value of £87.

This report caused the police much concern as they had never previously had a robbery on this road. It was referred to as 'highway robbery' and given a priority score of 16. The following day the police questioned some men in connection with another case (Nos 117 and 118) who admitted having robbed a man from whom they stole property corresponding to that lost by Alistair. He was asked to return to the police station and was reinterviewed by two detectives. After persistent questioning he began to reply with questions like 'What can a man do whose mother-in-law lives in a posh area, whose wife reads the local paper, who has just got a local authority job and doesn't want to lose it?' The police asked 'Do you realize that you were the first in a series of violent robberies in which other people also had knives held to their throats and that if you'd told the truth to start with then these other crimes might have been prevented?'. To this he replied 'My God! I've never thought of that. You're right. If I tell you the truth will you want to use it in evidence?' The police said that was something he should not take into consideration. If he was called to court he could make excuses to his wife and his boss and take a chance on whether it got into the paper. He said he thought his wife would understand if he told her, because his behaviour was out of character. He was just curious and might not have had sexual relations with a prostitute anyway. However, he was not sure whether his mother-in-law would believe him.

Alistair then made a second statement in which he said he was feeling depressed and had heard that St. Pauls was a red light area. As he drove along Ashley Road he saw two girls standing at a corner. He stopped his car and after only a few seconds one of the girls approached the passenger side; he opened the window and she asked 'Do you want business?' He asked 'How much?'; she said 'Ten Pounds'. He said 'O.K.' so she and her friend got in and directed him to drive round and round until they came to Chelsea Road. He followed them down a dark alley and into a house where, after handing over £10, he lost contact with the women. Later he left, but on the way out was punched in the stomach by a youth and then pushed against a wall by a second who held a knife to his throat and robbed him. The outcome of this case is described in Chapter Four.

120. Michael R., 14 years, was walking in the street with a £1 note in his hand when a group of youths came up, pushed him, and took the note.

127. Maurice L., 27 years, was attacked near the city centre at 0225 and property worth £50 taken from him.

129. Lewis S., 19 years, at 2035 in an underpass, was robbed by 4 youths of £51. When interviewed shortly afterwards he was unable to describe the robbers but several days later, after he had collected his thoughts, provided good descriptions. He was shown photographs without result. The detective noted 'the area of the attack is isolated and is the ideal place for this type of offence'.

130. John M., 33 years, at 2200 on Kingsdown Parade, was approached from behind by 4 young men; 3 restrained him while the fourth went through his pockets and took £65-50. A policeman toured the area

with him and an hour later he pointed out a man as responsible. This man was arrested but no other evidence against him was found and a witness testified that he was elsewhere at the time in question.

134. Alan C., 21 years, at 2200, was jumped upon by 3 youths who robbed him of £24.

137. Peter R., 47 years, at 1830 in a block of flats, was robbed at knifepoint of 90p.

141. Raymond C., 59 years, while in a car park at 1415 was grabbed from behind while a second assailant took £13 from him.

143. David B., at 2245 was attacked and struck by two men who robbed him of £800 in money. Interviewed next day, the complainant appeared to be of very low intelligence. Enquiries revealed that David had a cheque for £1,000 which he said was payment for work he had done. He had arranged with the landlord of a pub to cash it for him. The landlord gave him £800. Anonymous information was received that the two robbers were named men living rough in a nearby house. One was arrested but after interview eliminated. It transpired that the the cheque was one David acquired by deception from his landlady. He was convicted of deception at the Magistrates' Courts in respect of this but still maintained, probably truthfully, that he had been robbed as originally reported. Extensive enquiries were made but were without result three months later.

149. Colin G., 38 years, was in a park at 2300 looking for a lost dog when he was struck and robbed of £45. He is a man with a criminal record who is prone to exaggeration and is considered unreliable as a witness.

154. Charles G., 56 years, was held up in an underpass at 1935 hours and robbed of £50.

155. Richard S., 34 years, leaving the Black and White Cafe at 0030, was jostled by about 6 youths and £175 taken from him. He was shown photographs but could make no identification. The woman who was with him at the time was interviewed without result.

156. Peter M., a pensioner, at 2030, was grabbed from behind while in the street and robbed of £20 by two

youths whom he could not identify.

157. Shamshir S., 35 years, at 0210 was approached by two youths who threatened him with a knife and hit him on his back with a stick. The detective reported that the complainant refused to make any statement, to come and study photographs, or to help in any way. Attempts to make contact with him both by personal calls at his home address, and by telephone, had been unavailing.

158. Neil P., 32 years, was leaving a hairdressers when two youths pushed him against a wall and snatched his wallet with £32. He doubted if he could recognize them again.

159. Steven B., 15 years, was standing in the street when he was approached by two youths. One of them snatched at his radio/cassette recorder and, after a struggle, ran off with it. The police spent $9\frac{1}{2}$ hours with him (including the time spent touring the area and showing him photographs), 2 hours on house to house enquiries, 2 hours at the scene and 3 hours with witnesses. One youth answering to one of the descriptions, when being questioned in connection with burglaries for which he was subsequently convicted, admitted having been present at this robbery. His friend (whom he would not identify) had knocked the victim's arm in order to snatch the radio/cassette recorder and the two had shared the proceeds. When sentenced for burglary he admitted this offence as a theft and it was taken into consideration in the sentence. The police are still looking for the other youth responsible for the robbery.

STREET ROBBERIES OF FEMALES, INDEPENDENT EVIDENCE AVAILABLE

Eight cases of such robberies were reported.

5. Linda B., 29 years, was approached by two youths who pushed her against the wall and snatched her handbag containing property worth £50. One witness verified the report but could make no identification, and no one else came forward though in view of the hour many must have been passing. The victim was shown photographs but could not recognize anyone. Some paper from her bag was recovered; it was examined for fingerprints, unsuccessfully. An anonymous phone

call was received shortly afterwards saying that Roy Y. was responsible, but no trace could be found of such a person.

12.   Carol B., 19 years, at 1345 was walking along the same street as that mentioned in the previous case when 3 black youths came up, one of whom pulled from her neck a gold necklace worth £200 and went off with it.   Neither the victim, nor her mother, nor another woman who was with them could recognize the man.   They were shown photographs without result.   The detective said that to a lot of white people all black men look the same.   Over 11 hours were spent on the case because there were witnesses, including two black men who had been working nearby but without any identification.   To one detective it appeared to be an offence motivated more by bravado than by a desire for gain.

22.   Miriam B. 57 years, with a friend was crossing a footbridge over the motorway at 2205 on their way from church. They passed two youths. Later she was pushed to the ground, apparently in an attempt to steal her handbag.   The incident was not reported until 50 minutes later and the handbag was not suitable for finger-printing.

23.   Suzanne C., 29 years, a visitor from South Wales, went with a friend to a West Indian club.   Inside they were involved in a dispute.   On leaving they found that the window of their car had been broken, property stolen, and a corrosive liquid poured over the interior.   While they were inspecting the damage a man came up and snatched from her a gold bracelet valued at £200.   The area was searched and photos shown, without result.

A detective later recognized the description as fitting Donald R., arrested in connection with cases 8 and 15, who, while on bail, had been snatching purses in Broadmead, had been apprehended, and had made admissions.   Interviewed about this incident he denied involvement in it.   Told that he would be put on an identity parade, he admitted having been present but said someone else had taken the bracelet and handed it to him.   Eventually he admitted responsibility and made a written admission. He was charged with theft though this was technically a robbery.   It was dealt with when he was sentenced for other offences, as described in Chapter Three.

57.   Sarah H., 37 years, was walking with her husband at 2345 when two youths jostled them and one snatched her bag containing cash and property to a value of £10.   The complainant and her husband were both the worse for drink and they thought it more important first to 'knock up a pub and have some brandies' before coming to the police.

99.   Eleanor W., 32 years, stopped at an Indian takeaway restaurant.   While returning to her car, her shoulders were grabbed from behind and then a second man grasped her shoulder bag.   She was pulled to the ground, losing her bag.   Two days later a woman from St. Pauls was arrested in Gloucester for trying to obtain goods with one of the credit cards stolen on this occasion.   The man accompanying her escaped. This woman gave different names, claiming after a while that she got the card 'to order' from a named woman in St. Pauls.   That woman was arrested and her flat searched, unsuccessfully.   Some three days were spent investigating the background to the fraudulent use of the card.   The police became convinced that it had been obtained from Michael M.   He was put on an identity parade.   The victim of the robbery hesitated about identifying him.   Afterwards she said she was 'pretty sure' he was the one but could not be 100 per cent certain.

The woman who used the stolen card is Sylvia T.   While in custody she made telephone calls to two families in the West Midlands.   Records of fingerprints of some people in these families were held in police records and could be compared with impressions taken from the cheques, but without result.   Anonymous information about a car used in a robbery was also received but proved unhelpful and the detective thought it had been supplied to throw him off Michael M's trail.   Sylvia was indicted at Gloucester Crown Court on 3 February 1984 on charges of receiving stolen property and obtaining goods by deception.   11 additional offences were taken into account when she was made subject to a Probation Order for two years.

135.   Denise S., 36 years, was in Kingsdown Parade at 2210 when a man asked her for money.   She screamed; he put a hand over her mouth, tripped her up, and then ran off.   The police found the complainant a little 'odd', and her account of events confused. She could not identify the man.   House to house enquiries found neighbours who saw the assailant running off, but

could provide no description of him.

144.   Karen S., 16 years, was with her boy friend some time between 1430 and 1800 when she was held against a wall by a man who demanded money from her.   She reported this 4 days later.   The man, who was vaguely known to the pair, was identified as Derek A.; he was prosecuted and, after pleading guilty to theft, made subject to a Probation Order for 12 months and ordered to pay £20 costs.

STREET ROBBERIES OF FEMALES, NO INDEPENDENT EVIDENCE AVAILABLE.

Only one of these 7 cases was detected, and in that instance the offender was identified straight away by the victim.

114.   Alice L., 18 years, at 1700 was approached by a former boyfriend who tried to force her to walk with him and then kept saying he would like to wear her gold chains (worth £169).   Then he said 'Give me your chains or I will hit you'.   He took them and said she could have them back the next day whereas she wanted them back immediately and went to the police.   The police spent 6 hours interviewing the complainant, 4 hours talking to witnesses, 14 hours investigating, arresting and interviewing the suspect, 4 hours preparing case papers, 4 hours in court for remands, 3 hours for the committal and a further period for the trial.   The magistrates dismissed the robbery charge but committed the accused on other charges to the Crown Court where he was sentenced to 11 months youth custody.

7.   Sadie W., 24 years, was in Cathedral Square at 1400 when someone grabbed her from behind round the neck, put a hand over her mouth, and demanded money. He was disturbed before he was able to take anything. She was shown photographs without result, and asked to contact the police should she see the man again.

48.   Florence P., 76 years, at 2150 was returning from the pub when two youths, said to be one coloured and one white, pushed her to the ground and stole her bag. Her arm was broken.   A motorist saw her on the ground but saw no one run away.   The victim thought the coloured youth was the boy friend of a girl in her street so the police interviewed both the girl and her friend without useful result.   The detective, who put

13 hours into the case, came to believe that there had been no robbery. The complainant was known to drink a bit too much and to have fallen on other occasions. She was rather confused in her thought. She said she had with her a shopping bag and the handbag reported stolen. Others who saw her in the pub said she had only the former. The coloured youth she identified is Spanish and the only coloured person she knows. People who were around at the time and place where she says she was attacked saw and heard nothing. She may have reported or imagined a robbery to cover her embarrassment.

49. Josephine R., 41 years, while walking through an underpass at 1015 was hit in the back by a youth who tried to steal her handbag; meeting resistance, he ran off. She would not be able to recognise him. Reinterviewed later, she was confident about her first account but could offer no new evidence.

50. Jean B., 37 years, at 1500 was opening her door when her purse with £8 was grabbed from behind and she was pushed to the ground. She did not see her attacker's face. The detective described her as 'a sad little lady'. She had been looking after her recently deceased father and has gone to pieces because of his death, being already white-haired and stooping. The detective would have liked to do more to help her, but was stymied by the lack of any identification.

136. Rosie B., 21 years, at 1925 was approached by a young woman who struck her across the face three times and attempted, unsuccessfully, to snatch her handbag.

STREET ROBBERIES, KNOWN CARRIERS OF CASH

Of the 15 cases in this category, one resulted in a conviction, in 2 cases the police believed they knew who was responsible but could not assemble sufficient evidence, in 9 cases the reports had to be filed because of the difficulty of identifying any offender, while in at least 3 cases there were doubts about the genuineness of the report. Taking them in this order, these were:

33. At 1305 two employees of the South Western Electricity Board had just finished collecting money from electricity meters when they were attacked by 4 or 5 youths who stole their money bags containing

about £750. Several people saw the incident but only two or three were willing to give the police information. One witness identified one of the participants and could say where he lived. This information was available in 20 minutes. A Superintendant's warrant to search the premises of the suspect was obtained. He was no longer there, but £395, half the proceeds, was found. This man, Jonathan W., was arrested two months later. He had been living with his girlfriend in another neighbourhood. They had a dispute, and he went off with their daughter. The girlfriend notified the police and Jonathan was stopped at the railway station. He was then found to be 'wanted' for the robbery, arrested, allowed to consult a solicitor and interviewed. He made a statement in which he said that he and four friends saw the two men counting their money, the bags being on the floor. A friend grabbed one bag and he the other. No threats were made or violence used. At Bristol Crown Court he was sentenced to two years youth custody for theft (which is all he admitted to, and there was no other evidence to sustain the more serious charge). He would not name anyone else involved.

Information indicated that another participant might be Davidson W.; he had been seen in the area. Arrested, he denied participation, saying he saw it happen but that he recognized none of the participants.

Uniformed officers spent $19\frac{1}{2}$ hours on this enquiry, many of them at the scene of the offence. Detectives spent 15 hours in parallel plus a further 15 on the arrest and interviewing of Jonathan and 9 hours with the other suspect.

A detective at the station who knew something of this case had only recently been transferred to this sub-division and found it very different from the areas of which he had previous experience. People in this neighbourhood were much more unwilling, he said, to be seen talking to the police, to make written statements, or allow themselves to be identified. One man he had been trying to question had just asked him 'How many of you policemen live in St. Pauls? If you lived here would you give information to the police? You could easily find a fire burning at your front door and another at the back while your family was in the house'.

3.   Jeffery T., 46 years, is a turf accountant who at 1745 was taking £600 in a briefcase to his car.   He was punched so that he fell and hit his face on the ground.   Two youths were seen to run across the park with a briefcase.   Two elderly men (one black, one white) who probably witnessed the assault gave the victim the number of a suspect car.   The police attended, with dog handlers, and made house to house enquiries without result.   A car was traced, two youths found in it were arrested, and one detained. This youth was known to the bookmaker who said he was not involved, so he was released.   Two other men were arrested on suspicion but later eliminated.   The victim's briefcase was recovered without the cash.   No fingerprints could be obtained from it.   The victim compiled a photo-fit of his attacker but this did not help when appeals were made, via the press, for information from the public.   An identity parade was held to see if the victim would identify Donald R. (arrested in case 15); he was unable to identify anyone though the police remained convinced that it was he.   He was suspected of having robbed a jeweller in London in the same way.   He matched the photofit and information from informants associated him with the robbery.

Uniformed officers spent $2\frac{1}{2}$ hours, and detectives 10 hours on the case.   A further 7 hours were spent on the arrest and interviewing of 3 suspects.

148.   George B., 35 years, at 1045 was carrying £1,085 wages from the bank to a building site when he was approached from behind, knocked off-balance, and had the bag taken.   Two men ran off with it and were seen getting into a car.   The registration number was taken by a witness and it transpired that the car had been stolen during the preceding hour.   House to house and other enquiries were undertaken.   Two days later a man told a detective that two named individuals, Bruce and Leslie, had approached him earlier asking him to drive a wages snatch on the relevant date.   The addresses of the two men were available from other sources.   A search warrant was obtained and executed without result; the men were arrested.   Bruce corresponded to the photo-fit impression.   The men were interviewed. They had alibis for the time in question which were checked and found to be in order so they were released as 'refused charge'.

Following   an   appeal   through   press   and   radio,   the missing car was located, with an empty briefcase, but scenes-of-crime examination of the car and case proved negative. Uniformed officers spent 8 hours on the case, detectives 29 hours plus a further 29 interviewing the suspects separately. They remained convinced that these two were in fact responsible.

11. Dennis C., 48 years, left his printing works with £550 in a bag to take to the bank. At 1630 he was getting into his car ready to drive off when a youth looked through the passenger's window, knocked, and came round to the driver's door. Dennis managed to pull this door shut but was punched on the shoulder through the open window. Another youth was standing by. Dennis drove off but did not report the attempted robbery for another two hours by which time it was no use searching the area. He was shown photographs without result.

20. David B., 47 years, collects rents from residents in council accommodation. At 1005 one morning he was accosted by two youths, pushed against a wall and searched. He dropped a wallet containing £200 of rent money but the youths, not realizing what was in it, ignored it. Two witnesses appeared and the youths ran off. The area was searched and the witnesses shown photographs, with negative results.

24. Michael B., 55 years, is an insurance agent who collects premiums from customers. At 1820 one day he was forcibly searched by two youths and robbed of £7. The offence was reported immediately. Photographs were shown without any identification being made.

30. The barwoman at the Trinity Hall Community Centre normally deposits the night's takings in the night safe at the bank in Baldwin Street. On the night in question she was delayed. Two men offered her a lift. They stopped some distance from the bank. The barwoman walked along with the wallet containing about £830 when she was knocked down and the bag snatched. One of the men who gave her a lift was the club doorman. When interviewed, he gave false information which drew suspicion onto him, but no further progress could be made with the investigation and after 7 hours it was left aside.

53. Robert W., 62 years, is another insurance agent. At 1745 one afternoon, while on the landing of a block of flats, he was surrounded by 7 youths who took a

total of approximately £250 from him. There were no witnesses. A check of photographs produced nothing but the detective believed the complaint genuine.

67. James S., 47 years, was selling watches door to door whan at 1830 he was set upon by 5-7 youths who robbed him of property worth £270. Police searched the scene, carried out house to house enquiries, showed photographs, all to no avail.

69. Kenneth G., 28 years, was collecting money for a lottery organized by Bristol Rovers Football Club when two young men threatened to 'do him over' and took £18 from him. He was shown photographs but was unsure of his ability to recognize the men. Later 5 arrests were made but as no connection could be established the men were released.

74. Every morning, Mrs. Daisy P. goes from Iceland Frozen Foods with the previous day's takings to the local Post Office. On this occasion she was accompanied by a young assisstant (described by the police as 'far from bright'). On the way, at 1045, a man in his early twenties jumped on them, snatched the bag containing £3,700 in cash and ran off. Those attacked said he was about 5' 2". A house to house enquiry found witnesses who said the man was about 6'. One named a suspect, who was arrested. Another neighbour who had seen the incident testified that it was not him. Employees, past and present, were interviewed. 18½ hours were spent on the enquiry.

133. Patrick W., 41 years, collects cash on behalf of Shopacheck Ltd. At 1750 one day he was robbed of £80. Police searched the scene, toured the area with the aggrieved, showed photos, etc. without result. 20 hours were spent on this.

142. Arnold L., 28 years, is a street vendor who says he lent another man £3, holding his watch as security. The man returned for his watch and wounded the aggrieved, with a knife, stealing £25 from him. Police arranged for Arnold attend and have his injury photographed. He did not do so and other attempts to contact him failed. There seemed to be more to the dispute than Arnold had declared and the other man, when located, gave a different version. The complaint was eventually withdrawn. 15½ hours were devoted to it.

151.   Terry S., 39 years, collects money for a Cancer and Polio Research Fund.   At 2000 one day he had his head pushed into a wall and, he says, £100 stolen. The regional controller of the Fund doubted the veracity of the report, Terry having made a similar allegation previously and having afterwards come forward with the money.   The police reinterviewed Terry and, being dissatisfied, arrested him on suspicion of having misappropriated some or all of the money.   They did not get sufficient evidence to charge him and he was released, the police having spent 5 hours on the case.

153.   James S., 48 years, is the same watch salesman as in case 67; he reported that at 2300 he was grabbed by 3 youths and watches to the value of £1,327 stolen from him.   Witnesses spoke of two youths who were probably responsible but they could not be identified. 14½ hours were spent on this.   Later information was supplied by a neighbouring force.   A watch had been sent as a present to a relative of John G. (see case no 85 regarding an alcoholic).   The relative had taken it to the local police for them to enquire if it has been lawfully obtained.   John was interviewed but without result.

3 Robberies in shops and houses

Allegations of robberies in shops and houses may be weak as to details, but there is ususally no reason to doubt that offences actually occurred. These reports are therefore best classified not in terms of the evidence available to the police but in terms of their seriousness. The best indication of this is the weapon used, so that is the criterion on which Table 11 is based. The first column reflects the initial report, so that he 'pointed at her head what appeared to be a pistol type firearm' is counted as an armed robbery even though there may later have been dispute about whether it was really a gun. Tables 12 and 13 summarise information as to the times of day when the robberies were committed and the intervals before the police learned of them. In the case of institutional victims, like shops and banks, it is of no particular value to record the age of the person approached by the robber, so no table of victim's age has been prepared for indoor robberies.

Comparing these tables with those for street robberies it will be noticed that while there is a predictable tendency for robberies of shops to occur during business hours, and robberies of filling stations outside these hours, there is nevertheless a round-the-clock distribution. Indoor robberies (and attempted robberies, in which nothing of value was taken) are reported more quickly than street robberies. Some of them (especially the robberies of customers inside shops) differ

Table 11
Indoor robberies, by weapon and type of premises

Weapon	Shops Robbery of:		Houses	Filling Station	Post Offices, Banks, etc.
	Customer	Shop			
No weapon	2	3	1	1	1
Knife, etc	–	5	3	2	–
Gun	–	–	–	1	4

Note: one robbery of a customer occurred in a private house being used for commercial purposes and has therefore been counted as a shop. Of the 10 cases in line two, a knife was used in 8 and a stick and crow bar in the remaining two.

Table 12
Indoor robberies, by time

	Shops	Houses	Filling Stations	Post Offices & Banks
0000–0159	1	1	–	–
0200–0359	–	1	–	–
0400–0559	1	–	1	–
0600–0759	1	–	–	–
0800–0959	–	–	–	3
1000–1159	1	–	–	–
1200–1359	1	–	–	–
1400–1559	2	1	1	1
1600–1759	1	1	–	–
1800–1959	1	–	1	1
2000–2159	–	–	1	–
2200–2359	1	–	–	–

Table 13
Indoor robberies, by reporting interval

Interval	Shops	Houses	Filling Stations	Post Offices & Banks
Less than 30 mins	8	2	4	5
Within 2 hours	2	1	–	–
Within 12 hours	–	1	–	–
Within 24 hours	–	–	–	–
Over 24 hours	–	–	–	–

Table 14
Indoor robberies, by alleged loss

	Shops, Robbery of		Houses	Filling Stations	Post Offices & Banks
Loss	Customer	Shop			
nil	–	2	2	–	2
less than £10	–	2	–	–	–
£10–99	2	2	1	2	–
£100–499	–	1	–	2	–
£500–999	–	–	1	–	1
£1,000 plus	–	1	–	–	2

Table 15
Indoor robberies, by screening scores

	Shops, Robbery of		Houses	Filling Stations	Post Offices & Banks
Score	Customer	Shop			
0–3	–	–	–	–	–
4–6	2	2	–	1	–
7–9	–	1	–	1	–
10–12	–	2	2	–	–
13–15	–	1	–	1	–
16–18	–	1	1	–	–
above 18	–	1	1	1	5

Table 16
Indoor robberies, by hours in investigation

	Shops, Robbery of		Houses	Filling Stations	Post Offices & Banks
Hours	Customer	Shop			
0–5	–	–	–	–	–
6–10	1	1	–	–	–
11–19	–	4	–	3	–
20–49	1	2	1	–	2
50 and above	–	1	3	1	3

Table 17
Indoor robberies, by outcome

Shops, Robbery of		Houses	Filling Stations	Post Offices & Banks
Customer	Shop			
Detected –	5	3	4	3
Suspect(s), but				
Undetected –	–	–	–	1
Filed 2	4	1	–	1

little from street robberies, while the quick snatch of money from a till, accompanied by threats, may be over in a few seconds and therefore offer only poor prospects of detection. Nevertheless many of these reports understandably receive high screening scores, are given many hours of investigators' time, and have a much higher detection rate than street robberies. It will be convenient to review these cases in the categories employed in the tables, starting with the least serious.

ROBBERIES OF CUSTOMERS IN SHOPS

110.   Peter H., 18 years, was in a 'shebeen', (an illegal drinking house) at 0530 when a man enquired 'Do you like birds?'.   He followed this man to another such house where he felt a hand touching his rear trousers pocket and looking round, saw a man with some £20 notes in his hand who smiled at him.   He then found that he had lost 4 such notes from that pocket but was too frightened to challenge the man.   After half an hour he left, and phoned the police.   They spent 6 hours on the case, but, having only a poor description to go on, soon filed the report.

150.   Mrs. Sandra T., 26 years, was in a laundrette at 1935 when two youths entered to use the telephone. Later she left her purse on the bench while putting a coin into the machine.   The two youths reappeared: one pushed her, snatched the purse, and ran off with his companion.   The police spent 22 hours on the case (mainly by detectives making enquiries in the locality). The report had then to be filed.

ROBBERIES OF SHOPKEEPERS

19.   Ali N., 13 years, at 1445 was minding his

father's shop when 3 youths entered, one asked to buy chocolate, and, when the till was opened, grabbed the high value notes from it. The second youth took some of the remaining notes though the boy slammed the till drawer shut on his hand. The first youth said 'I'll cut your throat if you shout' but the boy did shout, for his big brother, and the three ran off with a total of £136. The boy thought he might recognize the first youth but could not do so from the photographs he was shown. The police would have liked the shopkeeper to close his shop for a while so that a scenes-of-crime officer could look for fingerprints, but he was unwilling to do so. Informants later said that two named youths were responsible. They were arrested, held for a day and a half, and then released. The detectives suspected that they were being blamed by people who had a grudge against them and that they had nothing to do with the offence. While under arrest these two youths gave the police some information about a group who could have tried to put the blame on them and which contained two fifteen-year-olds whom the detectives suspected of having been the robbers. The police (who spent at least 15 hours on the case) had one finger print which could possibly prove useful but they thought the prospects of detection poor. The detectives commented that when adults are in custody it is often possible to build up a relationship with them through interviewing but fifteen-year-olds have to be interviewed in the presence of a parent and if in these circumstances they are unwilling to talk this brings that line of enquiry to a stop.

One year and nine months after the original offence Mr. N. senior again contacted the police to say that the youth responsible for the theft had re-appeared and once more subjected the N. family to harrassment. He provided sufficient identification for the police to arrest Clive R., 19 years, who, when interviewed, admitted responsibility for the original offence. He had just completed a 9 months youth custody sentence for robbery in which a woman's bag containing contents worth £40 had been forcibly taken from her. Although the original offence contained the necessary ingredients for a robbery charge he was prosecuted for the lesser offence of theft which can be dealt with in the Magistrates' Court. Since he had served a custodial sentence for the subsequent offence the magistrates dealt with him by imposing a conditional discharge.

40.   Mohammed H., 39 years, was looking after his store one day at 2230.   He had been pestered for months by a group of some five youths, including the two suspected of the previous offence.   When Mohammed was about to put groceries into his van a group of youths attacked him, threatening him with a knife. One tried to open the till, the others robbed him of £50.   Mohammed speaks little English and could make no identification from the photographs he was shown.   But the two youths just mentioned, Trevor G. and Lance H., both recently released after serving sentences in a Detention Centre, had been seen in the vicinity and were arrested on suspicion.   The mother of one of them offered an alibi before she knew the time of the offence.   The solicitors representing the two suspects refused to allow them to be put on an identity parade. They were released, being bailed to report to the police station at a time when many other local youths have to report.   The police then arranged for Mohammed and his son, to be in the vicinity, separately, each in the company of a police officer.   Both witnesses independently identified both suspects.   Uniformed police spent 3 hours responding to the initial report. Detectives spent 6 hours with the complainant, 2 on house to house, 1 on scene-of-crime investigation, 4 with witnesses, 1 arresting the suspects, 2 investigating their background, 6 interviewing each one, 5 arranging the street identification, and 12 hours preparing case papers.   In the Crown Court, Trevor was sentenced to 6 months youth custody; Lance, who was also charged with burglary and drugs offences was sentenced to 9 months youth custody.   The drugs charge arose because he had cannabis in his possession when he attended at the police station as a condition of bail.   The detective took this as a sign of confidence on his part that he could get away with offences.

41.   At 1500 one Monday afternoon two young men entered a fur shop, threatened the female assistants with a knife, tied them up, took furs worth some £20,000 which they placed in plastic bags and removed. The robbers tied up the shop assistants in a way that permitted them to get a good view of the offenders.

Suspicion fell on Donald R., 25 years, after he had been arrested for a subsequent Post Office robbery, and upon Alan Y., 20 years.   Their names were suggested by an informant.   Arrested, Alan agreed to go on an identity parade where he was picked out by the first of the shop assistants. He then refused to go on a parade before the second assistant but was identified by her at a confrontation. Donald, under arrest for the subsequent offence, refused to go on any parade but was identified by one witness at a confrontation.

Alan then co-operated with the police. He took them along a railway embankment to a place where he had been accustomed to hide stolen property including a double-barrelled shot-gun. He had stolen the gun from a car in Bristol but the owner had reported it as having been stolen in Bath (perhaps he did not wish to explain how he came to park his car in a red light district). Alan subsequently admitted participation in the Look Service Station robbery (case no 10) and the robbery outside the Dug Out (case 18) as well as this one. He told the police that Donald was also involved in these offences but would not make a witness statement to this effect. Why he should have co-operated so well the detectives did not understand.

The police spent 28 hours investigating the initial report and 18 hours with each of the offenders up to and including the time of their first appearance in court. They were unable to recover the missing furs. On conviction in the Crown Court both were imprisoned: Donald for a total of 4 years 2 months and Alan to youth custody for 3 years 6 months.

73. At 0610 one morning while a shop assistant was sorting out newspapers for delivery a man entered, stared at her in a unnerving manner, asked for cigarettes, and then, when offered a packet, said 'I have no money. Have you got a £50 note? Give me £50 or I'll break every bone in your body'. By this time she had sounded an alarm and people came to her assistance. They called 999. The police, acting on the description found the man in the area. Ernest S., 23 years, was charged. Three hours were spent on the initial report, 9 hours on dealing with the suspect and preparing case papers. Because of the accused's mental condition and the lack of corroborative evidence about his alleged behaviour, no evidence was offered when he appeared in court and the charge against him was dismissed.

81. At 0120 one morning two men entered the 'Lone Star Burger Bar', assaulted the female assistant and the manager, robbing them of £50-60. One was wielding

a stick. Photofit identifications of the robbers were circulated and enquiries made with other forces. 12 hours were spent on the report but no leads were found and it was filed.

87.   Philip A., 58 years, is a newsagent who was in his shop at 1245 when a man entered, claimed that he had been short-changed, and, when the shopkeeper denied this, punched him several times, leaving when he was given £4. 7½ hours were spent on the report but the offender could not be identified.

103.   At 1030 one morning a chemists' shop in the centre of the city reported that a young man had threatened the assistant with a long-bladed knife. She screamed. He tried to close the door and, failing to do so, ran off. 16 hours were spent in investigation, without result.

116.   Joginder S., 44 years, was in his shop at 1730 when two youths entered, took a bottle of brandy, and tried to leave. When the shopkeeper, helped by a customer, detained them, they punched him in the eye and threatened him with a knife. They left empty-handed. The police had been called and one constable recognized one of the offenders as they ran off. Jimmie M., 20 years, and a friend of his, Sidney T., 20 years were arrested and prosecuted. The police spent 20 hours on the initial report, 14 hours on one of the accused, and 9 hours on the other, not including time spent in court. The first accused was sentenced to 6 months youth custody and the second placed on probation for 3 years.

ROBBERIES IN HOUSES

57A.   Dalbir S., 43 years, was in bed at 0340 in the flat above his shop (which is also a sub-post office). He was awakened by two men, one with a two foot sword, the other with a knife. The first held the sword to the throat of the victim who made an excuse to get up, then pushed his attacker on to the bed. The sword snapped. With one part of it the victim then set about his assailant, cutting off part of his ear and wounding him about the shoulders. The man with the knife then fled. Having disarmed his attacker, the victim locked him in the bedroom and telephoned the police. The intruder, however, jumped from the window and made off.

47

Acting on the victim's description of his assailant the police put out a call for two men with Mohican haircuts but it turned out later that they were men who had been wearing stocking masks. The press and TV publicized the incident. Someone phoned with information concerning the man with the sword but though the caller would not give a name the police guessed who it was. When visited, the caller gave further details which led the police to Joseph C. who had been living locally under a false name. The other burglar was Anthony B. who fell under suspicion because he had earlier been working on the premises. Arrested, he denied involvement, but then said that the car used in the get-away had been sold by Joseph to return to Ireland. An extradition warrant was obtained and he was arrested in Fermoy. The court gave him bail for 14 days but he broke this and disappeared. He was later arrested, conveyed to Bristol and charged. He and Anthony were prosecuted not for robbery but for aggravated burglary, being each sentenced to 4 years imprisonment.

The police spent some 30 hours on the initial report, 35 hours on Anthony and 60 hours on Joseph, covering arrest, interviewing and preparation of case papers.

The victim, Dalbir S., was nominated by the Detective Inspector for an award from the Waley Cohen fund which exists to recognize service by members of the public in attempting to prevent crimes against the property of others. An award was approved and presented to him by the Chief Constable.

97.   Graham B., 66 years, was returning home one afternoon at 1630 when he met two men coming to his front door. They said they were 'from the Council, dealing with rent rebates'. He sent them away and did not open his door. Five minutes later the bell rang and he found them outside. They said they had come back to check. After a pause, they pushed their way in, assaulted and threatened the man by pulling a wire tight round his neck, robbed him of £25, tied him up with a gag in his mouth, and left. When he got free some three-quarters of an hour later, the victim phoned the bank to report the loss of his cheque book and the police to report the robbery. The police undertook house to house enquiries immediately. They found that an 80 year-old man opposite had seen it all and had noted the time although he had not reported it. Photographs were shown to the victim and

witnesses on the day of the offence. Some fingerprints were obtained in the house but as the robbers put socks over their hands the chances of fingerprint identification were not encouraging. This took 48 hours of police time. Two reasonably good descriptions of the robbers were built up but there were no other leads. The victim was badly shaken by the incident and planned to move house as a result.

Later a senior policeman from another division was drinking in a local public house when he heard that Jacky J. was trying to sell a watch. A local detective made enquiries but could learn no more about the would-be salesman other than that he came from Cornwall. Enquiries were made of the police in Cornwall who were able to supply details of someone matching the description with a copy of his finger prints. This made it possible to identify an imperfect print found in the house where the robbery had occurred. A watch had also been stolen. Details of the wanted suspect were circulated. Nine months after the original offence Jacob J. was arrested in connection with another matter and was found to be the one wanted for this robbery. Confronted with the evidence against him he admitted the offence and named his accomplice, Colin S., who also made an admission. One was sentenced to 2 years imprisonment and the other to 15 months.

126. This offence, recorded as a conspiracy to rob, related to no 121 already described in the Chapter II. The conspiracy was between two men, Milton and Andrew, charged with robbing a man called Hugh P. After that robbery they agreed to try and rob a man called William. When William opened his door to them at 0100 Andrew ran off, Milton entered the premises, robbed William of £27, and murdered him with a knife. For this he was sentenced to life imprisonment. Andrew was sentenced to 2 years imprisonment, the sentence being suspended.

139. Arthur W., 67 years, and his wife, 64 years, live in the sort of smart-looking house which is likely to attract the attention of burglars. At 1745 one day, two men forced their way into the house knocking both the owners down. The wife sustained injuries from the fall. The husband was hit with a crow bar. Rings were taken from their fingers, and the house ransacked for jewellery. Valuables worth some £700 were taken. The police spent over 58 hours

interviewing the victims, undertaking house to house enquiries, and speaking with dealers who might be invited to purchase the jewellery. They could make no progress on the case.

ROBBERIES AT FILLING STATIONS

10.   At 2150 one evening a 21 year old female forecourt attendant was on duty at the Look Service Station when a man came in to buy cigarettes. He grabbed her hand so as to pull her up to the partition, and then pointed a pistol at her head. She was obliged to open the door and let the man (and a second man who had appeared by this time) into the office, where they stole £155 in money. The police attended, with tracker dog and scenes of crime officer. They searched the area. The victim compiled a photo-fit of her attacker and looked through photographs of possible suspects.

The following day a telephone call was received from someone who had been suspicious about a car parked in that vicinity at the time.   A check of police records revealed a car belonging to a man called Christopher R. who had no convictions but was suspected of dealing in drugs in a minor way. He at first said that at the time in question his car was at a garage, but when the police tried to check this he admitted that this was not the truth.   He was arrested on suspicion of involvement in the robbery.   Interviewed after arrest, he first said he had lent the car to two acquaintances.   Reinterviewed the following morning he said 'I will tell the whole truth'.   While near the Black and White cafe he had been approached by two young men who asked for a 'taxi ride'.   When the car was in motion they directed him to the filling station and said they were going to 'do a job' there.   He drove to the back of the filling station and remained slumped down in the car until they returned.   He claimed to know nothing of any gun or of the method of the robbery.   He then drove them back to the cafe where they gave him £40 (£27 of which was recovered from his house).   The man thought that the one robber was called Tommy and was from London. The other could be called Alan; he thought that his girlfriend might know.

So his girl friend was brought to see Christopher in the police station.   She thought the man in question

50

might be Alan Y. Christopher looked through police photographs and identified someone whom the police knew to be Alan Y. He was located without difficulty and arrested. He denied involvement and advanced two alibis. When his home was searched, a coat and scarf were found which matched the description given by the victim of those worn by the second robber; a pair of tinted glasses of a particular shape was also found hidden between the mattresses in the baby's cot and these matched the description of glasses worn by the first robber. Alan was interviewed twice again without result. No fingerprint evidence was forthcoming. Since the only evidence on which to hold him was that of an alleged accomplice, he was released on bail. At this stage therefore, the position was that a man with no previous convictions was on bail awaiting committal proceedings while another man who had previous convictions for robbery and was probably one of the principals in the case under investigation was at liberty and likely to escape prosecution. One of the detectives concerned with the matter described Christopher as 'quite a nice bloke' and felt that the situation was inequitable.

Two weeks later the position looked different. Alan had been arrested on suspicion of participation in an armed robbery upon a post office (case 15). Donald R., arrested for the same post office raid, was probably Alan's companion on the previous occasion. He had presumably been the first robber in the glasses. Since much of Alan's face had been covered by a scarf it was little use putting him on an identity parade. Donald had admitted taking part in the filling station robbery and although he had subsequently withdrawn this admission, application would be made to prosecute him along with Christopher. There was still insufficient evidence to charge Alan for the filling station robbery. The prosecutor decided that there was insufficient evidence to proceed against Donald on this charge but applied for him to be held in custody for interviewing in connection with offences in London. The interviews yielded insufficient evidence on these matters so on his return to court no evidence was offered and he was discharged. This did not give him his liberty, since he was also wanted in London for failure to answer to bail. Returned to London, he was allowed bail again.

The following month Alan was arrested for a further offence and while in custody admitted to participation

51

in the filling station robbery and made a witness statement implicating Donald as his partner. Given bail, Alan then spoke of trying to retract his admission.

A little over nine months after the filling station robbery, Donald, Alan and Christopher appeared before the Crown Court, charged as follows:

Donald and Alan jointly: (1) robbing the fur shop of property worth £19,368; (2) robbing the filling station (to which Alan pleaded guilty); (3) wounding Leonard A. with a knife and causing him grievous bodily harm; (4) theft of £10.

Alan: (1) dishonest retention of a stolen shotgun; (2) committing an offence while on parole from borstal training.

Christopher, jointly with Donald and Alan; robbing the filling station.

The police told me that at lunch time on the day of the trial they proposed, through counsel, that the charge against Christopher be dropped if he would plead guilty to receiving £40 (his share of the robbery proceeds). He did so, and the judge placed him on probation for two years. The police proposed this to be fair to him: without his help they would not have got so close to Alan, and through him, to Donald; their knowledge of Donald had then enabled them to detect the robbery of the fur shop. The police thought that they were being lenient and that they did not always get the credit when they reduced or dropped charges. The detective said that the defence lawyers did everything they could for their clients. The one person who was not represented in court was the victim, a poor girl who had a gun shoved into her face and her arm painfully twisted. The only recognition of her part in the event would be a formal letter to her employer telling him of the outcome of the proceedings.

At the trial there was a dispute about the identification because of a minor error. Immediately after the parade the accused had challenged the identification, saying that it would have been possible for the witness to see a paper in the inspector's hand and from this to deduce his position in the line. The inspector should have recorded this as an objection but instead he cancelled the parade. In the event the jury failed to agree; a retrial was ordered; it resulted in conviction. Donald was sentenced to a total of 4 years and 2 months imprisonment; Alan to a total of 3½ years youth custody.

Donald appealed against conviction on the grounds that the identification evidence had been unsatisfactory. He was released from custody pending a hearing of his appeal. The circumstances are discussed in Chapter Six. In view of the nature of this investigation the record of time expended by the police may be incomplete. It includes 7 hours by uniformed officers and 15 hours by detectives responding to the initial report; 39 hours dealing with Christopher and preparing case papers relating to him; a little over 60 hours with Alan (though excluding preparation of case papers) and an uncertain length of time dealing with Donald who was being investigated simultaneously for a series of offences.

21. At 1941 one evening the attendant at another filling station was approached by a man who threatened her with a carving knife. He wanted her to open the safe. She could not do this. He took £80 from the till, put it in a plastic bag and made off. A 999 call brought the uniformed police and CID who searched the area. An identikit portrait was composed and photographs shown without any positive result. It was recollected that there had been a similar robbery at the same place five months previously which remained undetected.

Six weeks later Matthew F. came to the police station and surrendered for three filling station robberies including one with a loaded shot gun. He said that he was afraid that if he went on he might hurt someone. He admitted to other burglaries and to 'taking and driving away' offences all over the country. He was remanded in custody to facilitate further enquiries, including some in London. Subsequently it transpired that the London detectives were less interested in Matthew than in his accomplices. These might have been putting him under pressure to continue with them so that he decided to surrender instead. He was sentenced to a total of 3 years imprisonment.

43. At 1415 an offender entered the shop premises of the filling station at Temple Gate, threatened the

53

attendant, and made her stay in the kitchen section while he stole £49 from the till. When shown photographs she picked out a particular man. The police circulated his description. He was arrested in Preston, brought back to Bristol, and a statement taken. He advanced an alibi which, when checked, was found to be correct so the suspect was released. The police had spent a little over six hours responding to the initial report and 10 hours dealing with the suspect. Then, less than 3 months after the robbery, the attendant saw a man going into a betting shop whom she recognized as the offender. She called the police who came and arrested him. Questioned, he admitted to having put the attendant in fear in order to rob the filling station. Convicted of robbery, he was sentenced to 15 months imprisonment.

71. At 0445 a man, described as being 'of Italian appearance' and accompanied by two others, entered a filling station. He kicked open the door to the office and, holding a knife to the attendant's throat, threatened to kill him should he move. The robber seized £111 from the till and ran off with his companions, one of whom the attendant remembered from his schooldays. The police spent $7\frac{1}{2}$ hours on the initial phase of the enquiry. The victim identified from photographs a man of Spanish birth called Roberto B. On previous occasions he has admitted many offences to a particular detective but is disinclined to talk with other policemen. Interviewed by the detective who knows him he made a statement admitting the offence in which he said 'I never hurt the man, but I got frightened when he pretended to be hurt. We only got £13 each; no way was there more than £60-odd, like'. Dealing with him, including the preparation of papers, took 11 hours. Despite his admission he pleaded not guilty on arraignment. Convicted for this and a series of other offences he was sentenced to 3 years youth custody.

ROBBERIES OF POST OFFICES, BANKS, ETC.

8. At 1805 one Thursday a Post Office employee was preparing to deliver 97 wage packets containing £10,325 when he was confronted by a man in Post Office overalls carrying a mailbag who pushed him down and ran off with the money bag. The victim recognized his attacker as Alfred J., a former employee. Alfred's address was ascertained and, when he returned to it,

he was arrested by the police. He claimed that his sister, brother-in-law and wife would give him an alibi. When they did, they were arrested on suspicion of being involved in the robbery. They then retracted, saying that Alfred had told them he had committed a robbery. Alfred himself then made an admission, providing the police with a note addressed to another man who was keeping the proceeds. The money was recovered from various hiding places and took a long time to count. The man who was keeping the money was charged but the sister, brother-in-law and wife were released, charges having been refused. When Alfred's house was searched, more stolen property was recovered. Upon conviction, he was sentenced to two years imprisonment. The initial stage of the investigation took 24 hours of police time. Arresting, investigating and interviewing the offender took another 9 hours.

100. At 1515 one afternoon a man entered the office of the Nationwide Building Society. He walked up to a cashier, pushing a white polythene bag under the glass partition. He muttered something she did not understand. Then she heard him say 'Money in the bag!'. He opened his coat to reveal a handgun tucked into the waistband of his trousers. Placing his hand on the butt, he said 'Put the money in the bag!'. The cashier then started to fill the bag with money during which time the man pulled out the gun but did not point it at her. With some £400 in it, the bag was given back to him and he ran off into the shopping centre. The police spent 39 hours at the scene, 2 hours on photo-fit and showing photographs, and 3 hours communicating with other forces. They associated it with a nearly identical offence in Taunton and interviewed 3 men (one already in custody) suspected of offences which had something in common with this one, but all the possible suspects were eliminated and the case had to remain on file undetected.

15. At 0920 one morning Post Office employees were making a delivery to a Post Office in St. Pauls. As the first employee was crossing the pavement with the moneycase a man who appeared to be holding a rifle or double-barrelled shot gun ran up. He hit the delivery man across the top of his head with the stock of the gun. Nothing was stolen and two young men were seen to drive off in a red MGB.

It may be best to follow the events of this case from the police perspective, concentrating on some of the more significant activities.

At 0918: message received from Post Office 'One of our vans has been attacked in Lower Ashley Road. One of the crew has been hit over the head with a shot gun.'

0920: ambulance required.

0921: two youths have made off in a red MGB towards Grosvenor Road; they are known to be in possession of a sawn-off shot gun.

0925 from a police car: we are following a red MG in Portland Square.

0926: from same car; vehicle has been stopped; believed not be connected with robbery.

0927: check points set up at five main exit roads from city.

0933: vehicle resembling description of the one sought has been found abandoned in Morgan Street.

0933: witness in Morgan Street says that two men ran from the car towards the Burnell Drive flats. First witness of robbery telephoned with description of wanted men.

0934: doghandlers summoned.

0938: two units of armed police with body armour summoned.

0941: Detective Chief Superintendant and a press liaison officer en route to scene of crime.

0950: call for low loading vehicle to collect suspect car.

0955: firearms units en route.

0956: report of suspect entering Dockland Settlement; cover of rear of building requested.

1001: WDC en route to hospital to interview victim of attack.

1003: suspect at Dockland Settlement interviewed and eliminated from enquiry.

1012: suspect vehicle examined; no trace of weapon found.

1019: additional description obtained of the man who had the gun.

1020: description circulated of the suspects wanted.

1021: house to house enquiries in progress.

1028: check points stood down.

Information was received that 'Tommy from London' might be responsible for the robbery; that he had earlier been seen in the street outside the Black and White cafe with a shot gun before taking it into 136 City Road. This harmonized with the information from Christopher R. that he might be the man responsible for the Look Service Station robbery (10). Warrants were obtained for armed police to search for weapons at 136 City Road, at the house of Alan Y. (suspected of being an accomplice of Tommy from London in an earlier robbery), at the home of Alan's brother (since he had spoken about the guns to a third party, Gilbert F.) and in Gilbert's hotel room. The searches were carried out early on day two (8 February) and were negative.

On day three someone phoned to say that he had been speaking with a woman who knew of a man referred to Tommy who came from London. Later she identified herself. Subsequently the police searched a flat in City Road and obtained finger prints. After two and a half days they arrested a man who came there. As he fitted the description of the wanted man the firearms units were then stood down.

Since November the police had been in possession of a Jaguar car which had been used in a theft from a shop, pursued, and had crashed, the driver escaping. The 'word from the street' was that the car belonged to 'Tommy from London'; also that when he had been seen in the street with a shot gun he was accompanied by his friend Gilbert. So Gilbert was arrested on suspicion of involvement in the robbery. He was found to have 1 lb of cannabis under his bed. Gilbert said that Tommy had both a shot gun and a hand gun which he

57

thought might be a replica. He also believed Tommy to have been a party to the filling station robbery in which a hand gun had been produced. Since Gilbert's wife provided him with a credible alibi covering the time of the Post Office robbery he was eliminated from that enquiry.

The man arrested at the woman's flat on 11 February gave his name as Tommy R.; he allowed finger prints and a coloured photograph of himself to be taken. No gun or other evidence was found. From central records he was identified as Donald R., wanted in London for failure to appear in court to answer a charge of attempted theft and suspected by the police there of involvement in attempted robbery. Only at the end of his first day in custody would be admit his identity.

The police put pressure on Gilbert to help them locate the guns. They allowed him to speak to Donald in private. Donald was told that there would be an identification parade before witnesses to the post office and filling station robberies, and to the possession of firearms in the street. He said he did not want the woman from the service station to come. He would admit to responsibility for that offence. He said the hand gun was a toy: 'it's been mashed up'. He would make no statement before he had consulted a solicitor, which he did on the first day. (When asked why Donald should admit the one offence and not the other the detective replied that there was a 'Robin Hood element' in the filling station case for the attendant had asked the robbers not to take her handbag because it contained all the money she had and they had left it, whereas at the Post Office a firearm had been produced and a man injured so it would be regarded as more serious.)

On the second day in custody Donald admitted that he was the owner of the Jaguar car. On the same day he was put on an identity parade before eight witnesses: the victim in the post office robbery, and seven other people who reported having seen the robbery, or men they associated with the get-away car, or men seen apparently with a shot gun in the street where that car had been left. None of them identified Donald, who then told his solicitor that he retracted his admission to the filling station robbery. The police were running out of time for which they could detain him so he was charged with the filling station robbery. Produced in court the following day, the prosecutor felt unable to proceed on this charge and invited the bench to dismiss it. Donald was detained for interviewing and for breach of his bail. During the time of this remand he was put on another identification parade before the victim in the filling station robbery (10); the turf accountant robbed of £600 (3) and the man wounded in the car park robbery (14). None identified him, though the filling station attendant hesitated between him and another man before deciding that it was the other. The police also learned that immediately after the Post Office robbery their prisoner had been living at 26 Ludlow Close. This address had been visited during the house to house enquiries and Donald had been in the premises, but police had not enquired closely because they did not know that the tenancy was in new hands.

On the same day as Donald was first before the Bristol magistrates a friend of his called Richard M. was arrested. Donald had told Gilbert that the shot gun belonged to Richard. No gun was found at Richard's house and he denied knowledge of the offences. The charge against him was refused. By this time the police had a photograph of Donald. Together with 199 other photographs it was shown to a witness to one robbery who identified it, but said that he did not have the courage either to identify Donald in public or to testify against him because he feared for the safety of his girl friend and children.

As has already been mentioned in the description of the filling station and fur shop enquiries, Alan Y. had been an accomplice of Donald. He was arrested on suspicion of involvement in the Post Office robbery but released after interview. He had shown the police where the gun had been hidden. The police thought they knew who had been the get-away driver (a white man wearing a black mask). The principal offender in the Post Office robbery was going before the court anyway. To secure an additional conviction in respect of this offence was therefore not so important and they knew enough about it to be allowed to count it as a detected crime.

45 was a case involving much police activity but less detective work. At 1040 one morning two men, Sebastian K. and Donovan R., entered a bank in the city centre. Each carried a gun. They got behind the bank counter and, holding the staff at gun-point, stole £35,000 from the tills. They discharged a

sawn-off shot gun inside the bank. They then left the scene in a car closely pursued by police vehicles. Both men were seen to transfer to a Mercedes which was pursued and then trapped inside a factory compound area. Two policemen, knowing the robbers to be armed, nevertheless ran to the Mercedes and attempted to break its windows with their truncheons. The passenger fired at the one constable and missed. The driver apparently fired at the other, shooting him in the face, but forensic study showed that the bullet which nearly killed him came from the passenger's gun. The robbers then escaped and were pursued for 5 miles by a police motor cyclist whom they attempted to shoot. When a patrol car took up the chase, the robbers left their car and fired at the officers in the pursuit car in an attempt to hi-jack it. Fortunately the officers in that car had weapons. They had been engaged in a firearms operation earlier that morning in connection with a separate incident. They had been about to return their weapons to the armoury when news was received of the bank robbery. So two officers were able to shoot at their assailants. Donovan fell, still firing his pistol at the Sergeant, who shot again and the constable, showing personal bravery, managed to disarm him. Sebastian ran back to the Mercedes. To hinder his escape, a constable fired at the rear window. Some of the shot undoubtedly struck the driver because following his arrest he was taken to hospital with minor gun-shot injuries. The detective reporting on the enquiry wrote 'I have been unable to obtain a statement from the doctor who treated the injuries as he has declined to make a statement without the consent of the patient'.

The Mercedes raced away and crashed. The robber ran off taking a pillow case containing the money. Seeing a woman who had just left her car he threatened her with his gun, took her car keys, and drove off. This car was soon stopped by a police road block. The robber then ran off with a hand gun, this time leaving the money and a shot gun. Holding a gun to his head he tried to take a policeman as hostage but failed and ran off to a lorry where he forced the driver to drive him away. With the safety of the lorry driver uppermost in their minds, the police then allowed the lorry to be driven along the motorway for nearly one hundred miles to a point at which another road block had been established. Failing to crash through it, the vehicle was surrounded by armed policemen and the robber surrendered.

Interviewed by the Detective Superintendant, Sebastian made a statement amounting to a full admission. He claimed to have driven down from London that day but other evidence was assembled suggesting that the two men had been to Bristol on numerous previous occasions and that the robbery had been carefully planned. Both men were suspected of responsibility for bank robberies in the London area in which at least 8 persons had been shot. Sebastian was charged with (1) attempting to murder a policeman; (2) robbing a London bank of £1,750; (3) robbing another London bank of £13,881; (4) firing a shot gun with intent to prevent his arrest in connection with the previous offence; (5) robbing a Hertfordshire bank of £9,000; (6) stealing and unlawfully carrying away the lorry driver against his will. Donovan was charged with (7) attempting to murder the second policeman. The two were jointly charged (8 & 9) with robbing the Bristol bank of £35,108. Both men were convicted and sentenced to life imprisonment. Further charges, for other offences, were brought against them later.

145. The last of the armed robberies perpetrated during the year was recorded as a conspiracy to rob, and raised issues of a different kind. Properly to appreciate the sequence of events it would be necessary to explain the reasons the police had for taking an interest in the activities of four men, not all of whom had significant criminal records, and of the various sources of information about them. Since those sources have to be protected, the description of the case is abbreviated; little can be said about the difficulties of the police when deciding what they should do in the early period when they had reason to suspect a conspiracy but no robbery had been committed. For example: the suspects stole a car. Believing that firearms were to be used, the police decided that their main priority should be to recover these; therefore they should not at this stage arrest anyone for stealing the vehicle. When this car was left in a side road it was spotted as stolen by a patrolling policeman who had it removed, to the frustration of the detectives who had been watching it. Difficulties also arose because of events in a different police division which resulted in one of the suspects being arrested in connection with a separate matter, and so other people got drawn in and this created new problems for the detectives. To which

police station an arrested person is taken can be important when several criminals are working together because frequently two or more arrested men have to share a cell; information can leak out through other prisoners, other police officers, and through solicitors visiting clients, even without the parties realizing this.

From what they had heard the police suspected that a post office robbery in northeastern Bristol was possible, and prepared for this. Then the suspects drove off, in two vehicles, in quite a different direction and stopped in a wooded area. The police then learned that a Post Office van making a cash delivery was due to pass. They had to make an important decision: whether to allow the suspects to reach their target and arrest them as they commenced the robbery, thus ensuring that there was sufficient evidence to obtain a conviction, or to ambush the suspects at an early stage and arrest them before they attacked the vehicle. The first option might well have put innocent persons at risk, but adopting the second option had the disadvantage that the police might not be able to obtain sufficient evidence to charge the suspects who would then have been free to plan and commit further offences, possibly putting even more people at risk.

The police decided to stop the Post Office van and to close in on the stolen car. They were seen during the approach, and one of the suspects appeared with a shot gun. He fired a shot at the officers and made his escape from the scene together with the other men. The police attempted to put a ring around the area but because the majority of the officers had been deployed to the North East of Bristol, fresh officers had to be called in who had not attended any of the briefings and were insufficiently well informed about those they were to look for. So when two of the suspects stopped and gave false names they were not detained. Indeed, when eventually arrested, one of them asked 'We weren't the only wallies there on the day were we?'. In the stolen car a gun, coshes, face masks, ammonia and other things were found. Subsequently nine warrants to search for firearms were executed, but with little result. One suspect, Malcolm B., returned to his house in Bristol and was arrested. To none of the four questions the police put to him would he reply and the police did not want to question him further for fear of disclosing how much they knew and did not know about the circumstances. They did, however, give the names of the wanted men to the press and this paid off. Because someone passed on his suspicions to the local police, Arthur S., Reginald D., and Luke S. were arrested by armed police officers at a guest house on the south coast.

As the position was then described by a detective, matters did not look particularly promising. Arthur and Reginald were unlikely ever to make any voluntary statement. The detectives had put to them questions such as 'we believe there's a second gun. You could help yourself by telling us'. These questions, and any resulting answers, would probably be excluded from any trial as legally inadmissible but the police had no other way of indicating the sort of people they were dealing with. Luke had admitted driving the car and this could reduce any eventual sentence, but no-one could be sure the judge would see it that way. This detective felt depressed about the obstacles in their path and disliked the way they could make the police into hypocrites.

Reginald agreed to go on an identity parade and was picked out by six witnesses, but when Arthur was asked he at first agreed and then withdrew (contrary to his solicitor's advice). Nor would he agree to a parade in which the police would put similar looking men into his cell. All the police could do was to arrange for him to be identified while in his cell and at least he had not put a blanket over his head as some other prisoners had done. Since the identification evidence relating to Arthur was weak the DPP might decline to prosecute. The detective said that this would be heart-breaking because Arthur was a danger to society; in the last three weeks they had prosecuted more than a dozen 'idiots' for minor crimes – 'why put them inside and let these get away?'. He added that a lot of time and effort had been put into the investigation, and that had they allowed the robbery to go ahead the offenders would easily have been caught. The detective said that he felt frustrated not by the defendants' silence but by the trouble to which others had been put when they executed the search warrants, when they stopped lots of cars and told drivers (incorrectly but in good faith) that a policeman had been shot, and while they filled the prisons with 'puddens'.

The four defendants pleaded not guilty at their trial.

Three were convicted. Arthur was imprisoned for 7 years, Reginald for 6 and Luke for 4. The jury could not agree in the case against Malcolm. Since he had been held in custody for nearly ten months, it was decided not to ask for a new trial of the charges against him.

4 Other robberies

The action taken in connection with 26 other reports of robbery remains to be described. They were a mixed bag of cases. Though some of those already described were associated with prostitution and with drunkenness, there were others where the connections were so close that it is better to describe them separately. There were 14 cases of robbery directly connected with prostitution; 3 connected with drugs; 7 in which drunkenness was a major consideration; and 2 robberies which occurred in taxis.

PROSTITUTION

Taking first the 14 cases connected with prostitution, with one exception in all cases for which information is available the victims were males aged between 27 and 36 years and, apart from one dubious complaint, they all occurred during the hours of darkness. The alleged sums stolen varied between £5 and £286. In 10 of the cases information about the interval before reporting is available: 4 in less than 30 minutes, 3 more than than that but less than 2 hours, 2 more than that but less than 12 hours; and 1 less than 24 hours. Screening scores were: 0-3, 2; 4-6, 1; 7-9, 3; 13-15, 2; 16-18, 1; above 18, 3. Hours expended on investigation were: 0-5, 4; 6-10, 1; 11-19, 5; 20-49, 4. Seven of the cases were detected (the serious ones, with an average screening score just over 18); 2

cases were dubious reports; one should probably have been considered as a theft; 1 was withdrawn while the remaining 4 were filed. The cases can be considered in turn, starting with the dubious cases and concluding with those which were detected.

42. Albert F., 29 years, reported that he gave a lift to a woman he knew and then 'popped in for a cup of coffee with her'. While there two men burst in, pushed him on the bed, and stole £65. He said he had been robbed once before and thinks it may have been while in the company of this woman who is known as a prostitute. She remembered him as a bona fide client and said that he was not robbed while with her. The detective considered the report unreliable.

44. Charles C., aged 36, said that he went to the home of a woman he knows as Gabrielle whom he had previously paid for sexual interourse. She had friends with her. The two of them went to an off-licence, bought a bottle, and returned. As he was leaving he was set upon by 4 youths who robbed him of £90. Gabrielle confirmed the first part of his story but had heard of no robbery. His property was not recovered, so there were some doubts about his story.

104A. Two students from the Middle East reported that after leaving the flat of a prostitute they were attacked by youths who robbed them of £157. They showed the police which flat they had visited. They could not identify any suspects from the photographs they were shown. Because of possible embarrassment to their families should the circumstances be publicized, the aggrieved then withdrew their complaint and it was recorded as 'no crime' though the police believed the report to be genuine.

72. Brian B., 36 years, is a commercial representative who was staying over night in Bristol and who went to St. Pauls looking for a prostitute with whom he could 'do business' in his car. He picked up a woman who directed him to a back street where he parked. He had undone his trousers and pulled them down preparing to have sexual relations with the woman when a man appeared at the driver's window of the car. This man tried to open the door, then smashed the window with a hammer and reached inside to unlock it. He started to drag the first man from the car, pulling out the keys from the ignition, and then grabbing at his trousers. Eventually he was

able to tear them off and ran away with them, searching the pockets. The woman thought she saw the robber hit her client with the hammer so that blood began to spurt from his head. She was terrified and ran off to a call box, 'phoned the police, and then went back with them, being surprised to find that her client had gone. His only injuries had been grazes to his bottom when he was dragged along the road; there was no money to be stolen from his trousers. A statement was later taken from him. The woman thought she recognized the robber and named someone, but the police decided that he could not have been involved and discontinued their enquiries quite quickly.

104. Terrence G., 63 years, met two women in a night club. They agreed to let him come back with them and encouraged him to leave the premises on the pretext that they had a car nearby. As they went up a side street two men appeared: one held him while another robbed him of money and property to a value of £125. The police spent 29 hours on the case, including time spent on processing his papers (after recovery) for fingerprints and for a police officer to accompany the aggrieved while he kept observations outside the night club to see if any of the group returned. They drew a blank.

105 and 106, were two Danish workers aged 27 and 31, working at a site in the country. They came into Bristol by taxi, got drunk, and then went to look for prostitutes. Two women took them to several houses in St. Pauls where they had more to drink; while in the same locality they were robbed of £150 by a group of 4-5 youths. Both men were too drunk to interview properly and one spoke little English. They were taken on a tour of the area and shown photographs but there was never much chance of their being able to make any identification.

132. Two seamen from a Greek ship came to a night club. One was Egyptian, the other Indian, and they communicated in Greek. At the club they met two women with whom they drove early the following morning to a flat in an area they could not describe. The Egyptian paid in advance for sexual relations. Then there was a quarrel in which one woman (later identified by police enquiries) said she was assaulted by the Egyptian. She injured him with a knife. His trousers (which he was not wearing at the time of the quarrel) had disappeared from the room. When they were

recovered their owner said that US $170 was missing from them but there was no evidence that this had been taken after he left the club. The woman was arrested for wounding him though she alleged that she had acted only in self-defence. The police wanted to prosecute her immediately while their witness was still in port. Someone from the office of the solicitor defending the accused told the prosecuting solicitor that she would plead guilty so he did not resist a defence application for an adjournment. Then she changed her plea. Since the key witness had left and could not be brought back the prosecuting solicitor did not wish to apply for her to be committed to Crown Court, but the police insisted partly because they thought there had been an attempt to trick them. They said that the prostitutes in the area seemed to think that they could safely deceive foreigners. The police had not pursued the Danish workers' case because they had left Bristol, though perhaps this case could have been detected. This was the third case of the defrauding of foreigners visiting that particular club and the woman charged had a conviction for robbing a client. From the prosecuting solicitor's point of view however it was not a good use of public money to pursue a case when there was little chance of a conviction. When the accused appeared in court she agreed to be bound over in the sum of £50 to be of good behaviour and keep the peace for a period of one year. The police viewed this as a satisfactory outcome.

101. David E., 32 years, was with a prostitute at 0330; two men entered, threatened him with a knife and robbed him of £150. The police identified the woman from the description given. The victim alleged that she had arranged the robbery; she was at the time on probation for a like offence, but there was no evidence to support this interpretation and the men could not be identified. Two suspects were arrested but charges against them were refused. When the papers were forwarded to the prosecution department for proceedings against the woman alleging that she had participated in the robbery, a prosecuting solicitor advised against prosecution observing that there was no evidence that she had encouraged it. According to the victim's own statement she had said (of one of the intruders) 'What's he doing here?' and this implied the contrary. In the detective's statement about his interview with the woman he made what the solicitor called 'the unfortunate remark' that 'we are not the vice squad'; 'this is clearly an

inducement and may well render what follows inadmissible which would leave us without any identification evidence'. By the time the case came to court the police had instructed the prosecuting solicitor's department to offer no evidence, so the acccused was discharged.

65. John T., 34 years, met a woman in the street. Hearing that she was a prostitute, he came to an arrangement with her and they returned to her flat. There four drunken Irishmen, aided by the woman, assaulted him and threatened him with a knife, robbing him of £12.50. Later he saw one of them going into a pub, grappled with him and got back £10. He reported the offence to the police who went with him to the flat and found there a shoe which the aggrieved had lost when he fled. All five participants in the robbery were prosecuted but the aggrieved suffered a nervous breakdown and became unfit to testify, so at court the charges were dismissed.

117 & 118. Two 28 year-old brothers, Matthew and Mark J., went with prostitutes to an address in Chelsea Road. They gave money to the women who promptly left. The men were then robbed at knife-point by three youths, losing cash and property to the value of £286 and £157 respectively. They therefore took the police to the address in question and it was raided by the vice squad who arrested 3 men and 4 women. This part of the operation took 8 hours; time spent with each of those arrested varied between 19 and 9 hours each but it included the investigation of some other robberies: 113 Alistair H., described in Chapter II, 115 on an unknown person which the accused also admitted and asked to be taken into consideration, and 119, Bertram B. Bertram first alleged that he had been walking down the stairs in a block of flats when he was grabbed from behind by some young men and robbed of cash and property to a value of £83. Reinterviewed the following day, he made a new statement saying that he had picked up a prostitute in his car; she demanded £10 in advance. She led him down an alleyway, and into a house, leaving him in a room with two mattresses. She went out, was heard speaking with someone, re-entered, and said 'Someone else wants to use this room. You go and wait in the car and I'll be out in a minute'. By this time he was worried, and seized the opportunity to leave. In the alley way he was grabbed and something with a sharp point was held to his neck. There were three men, who robbed him of

the property previously described.

When the case papers were received in the office of the prosecuting solicitor it was noticed that the police wished to proceed against two brothers, Norman and Roger T., a third man Ian M., and two women called Phyllis S., and Margaret J. A fourth man, Neil L., had been interviewed but as the evidence against him was slender, he was not to be prosecuted. The prosecuting solicitor considered that there was no evidence that Ian had participated in robbery and no good reason to draw a distinction between him and Neil whom the police proposed should be called as a witness for the prosecution. If the police refused to drop the robbery change against him, it would be advisable to charge all five defendants with conspiracy to rob and see whether, at the committal proceedings, further evidence was educed in oral testimony. This was done.

Committal proceedings were delayed because on the first occasion the principal prosecution witnesses, Matthew and Mark, failed to appear. They were itinerant dealers and tarmac-layers and were not easily traced. A month later the hearings took place. One of them testified that there had been four men involved but he did not say that Ian had taken part in the robbery. All five were committed to the Crown Court on all charges. The prosecution solicitor represented to the police that Ian should be discharged and possibly used as a prosecution witness. This advice was not accepted.

When the case came before the Crown Court it had again to be postponed because the police had been allowed insufficient time to trace the first pair of brothers. The barrister who appeared for the prosecution took the view that the conspiracy charge could not be sustained against Ian so that he had to be discharged from the robbery case also. This left the brothers Norman and Roger and two women, Phyllis and Margaret, all charged with robbery. Phyllis had tried to plead guilty on her first appearance in the Crown Court. She was expecting a baby in a little over a month's time and preferred to have it in prison rather than to be sentenced after the baby was born, because in that event the baby would be taken into care were she sentenced to imprisonment. The judge observed that he could remand her in custody in which case she could have the baby in prison, but this did not appeal to Phyllis. When, two months later, her co-accused were tried, sentence on Phyllis was adjourned. Since the other woman, Margaret, was sentenced to perform 180 hours community service, and not to a term of imprisonment, it seemed that Phyllis had been wise to apply for a remand on bail. In the end she was made subject to a Probation Order for two years.

At the trial Matthew and Mark testified that they had seen one of the female accused in the street with an injured arm so they escorted her home out of chivalry. They insisted firmly on this version of events and were not shaken in cross-examination. They were both devout Catholics and what had made them determined on prosecution was that in the course of the robbery their wedding rings were taken. Alistair H. and Bertram B. testified. The former was very embarrassed but was probably relieved when there was no mention of the proceedings in the newspapers (the journalists were in another court listening to a case with greater news value). The accused had been asked if they wished the robbery of the unknown person to be admitted and taken into consideration in sentencing, but they retracted their previous admission and denied any knowledge of the case. Their defence consisted of an attempt to discredit the police witnesses and to persuade the court that their admissions in custody had not been made voluntarily. This failed. Norman, the elder of the brothers T., was sentenced to 3 years youth custody and Roger to 1 year. (It may be noted that it costs the public purse £840 per day to cover the cost of providing a Crown Court, including the building and staff salaries but not the fees of the prosecution and defence lawyers, and that this case took the better part of five days.)

DRUGS

In these three cases one man and two women were the victims. They were all reported within 45 minutes. The screening scores were 3, 4 and 8; the hours expended 1, 8 and 9. One was detected, one reclassified as 'no crime' and the third report filed.

13. John S., 44 years, was an assistant in a butcher's shop. A man was waiting outside the shop at 1500 one afternoon when he saw the till opened; he entered, pushed the assistant aside, and snatched £40. The police attended, spending less than two hours in the vicinity. Soon afterwards Kevin S., 35 years, a

registered addict, telephoned the police to say that he was responsible. After arrest and interview, he admitted this offence and the theft of 50 blank prescription forms. He is a drug addict who in the past has had dealings with a particular detective; it was this man whom he telephoned, saying that he wanted to talk and threatening suicide. Dealing with him took 7½ hours. He was prosecuted, not for robbery but for theft, and was placed on probation for two years, the order to run concurrently with a previous probation order.

92.   Sybil G., 33 years, is a woman who, at 2300, while under the influence of drink and drugs, was walking in the open in front of a block of flats. Two youths grabbed her, kicked her on the legs, and ran off with a handbag that was subsequently recovered. There was nothing in it of value. She could not describe the youths. The police searched the area but they had too little to go on.

111.   Rosemary S., 34 years, reported that at 0545 she was on the pavement walking towards the Black and White cafe when 5 youths surrounded her, knocked her down and took her handbag and other property to a value of £95. She telephoned the police. When interviewed shortly afterwards she said she had been out to buy 'weed' and that at the Blues Club she had been punched in the course of a domestic dispute. She had left there in 'a state' and it was shortly afterwards that the robbery occurred. It was possible that the culprits were known to her, if not directly, then through third parties, but she was unwilling or unable to describe the offenders. Throughout the interview the complainant was very agitated and appeared to be just coming down from a 'trip'. She was at times very abusive and at other times vague to the point of incoherence, being unable to concentrate. She declined to help any further. She was left the name and telephone number of the officer in the case and advised to contact him if she had any additional information. He tried to reinterview her several days later but could make no progress so the report was filed. Eight hours were spent on it.

DRUNKENNESS

In 7 of the 8 cases in this section the alleged victims were men. Four were reported within 2 hours but some of the others came to light only much later. The sums alleged stolen were relatively small but in some cases there were serious injuries, three of them being given screening scores of 20, 29 and 41; these took considerable time to investigate. The two most serious were detected. Four reports were withdrawn or reclassified as 'no crime'.

32 & 34. A man, Bruce H., 49 years, and a female companion, Kathleen B., said that at 0230 one morning they were attacked. He was held, his pockets searched, and £13 stolen. She was knocked to the ground and lost cash and property £10 in value. The constable who recorded the complaint viewed it with scepticism because both parties were drunk. The detective who interviewed them the following day was persuaded that the complaint was genuine though identification was lacking. Photographs were shown without result. Eight hours were spent on the case.

37. Patrick D., 36 years, met two vagrants and agreed to go with them to a room where a prostitute lived. They allegedly assaulted him, taking money from him to buy liquor which they drank together. Though he had apparently been a willing participant, the aggrieved reported them to the police to try to get his money back. He would not wait at the station to make a statement. The alleged offence occurred at 1500 and he was still drunk at 2330. When a detective went see him the following day he withdrew his complaint. The detective said 'we arrested two men for nothing. It was just a drinking party that went wrong'. The case was reclassified as 'no crime'.

66. Wallace S., 58 years, at 1900 one evening, was invited into a flat where a man pushed him to the ground and robbed him of £45. He was drunk and either too frightened of the other men around or disposed to make it up with them, because he withdrew his allegation although it was probably genuine. Six and half hours were spent talking with him and other people in the vicinity.

75. John D., 34 years, lived in the same block of flats as that referred to in the previous case. Two flats are occupied by men in an advanced state of alcoholic addiction. Three men were in one of them when John called for a drink. One man left the room and returned with a weapon with which he clubbed John. Someone else then stood on him. They removed his clothes, abstracting some £21. They then dragged him

to the bathroom and filled the bath three-quarters full with cold water. By this time there was a lot of blood about. They put him in the bath and tried to hold him under the water. John attempted to get out. He was then hit heavily and his leg broken badly. One of the others next befriended him and the following day called an ambulance. By this time he was within a few hours of death. After he had been in hospital for a few days he was willing to tell the police what had happened. Had this offence been detected earlier it would have been possible to prevent the occurrence of a subsequent offence (83, Peter McE.), since this involved some of the same men. The police spent $5\frac{1}{2}$ hours on the initial phase of the enquiry and $11\frac{1}{2}$ hours with the 3 men who had maltreated John. They were brought before the magistrates court for committal on a charge of causing grievous bodily harm but the evidence given against them by John was unsatisfactory and the cases were dismissed.

80.   Walter G., a retired man, reported that while in a toilet at a public house he was assaulted by unknown men who robbed him of £10 and personal papers. Enquiries indicated that he was drunk when he reached the public house.   He had staggered to the toilet and the next thing he knew was that he woke in hospital with injuries that were probably sustained in a fall. A search of his clothing uncovered the watch he had reported stolen.   The detective reported 'Walter has reviewed the situation rather philosophically and blames the 'demon drink'.'   It was reclassified as 'no crime'.

83.   Peter McE., 25 years, was a Scotsman who associated with the alcoholics mentioned above.   When he called there to drink with them they put into his glass some Chorol, a tranquilizing drug supplied on prescription to alcoholics to calm them down and help them sleep.   When he was unconscious they took from him £40.   Later they sat him on a wall, but when he 'looked bad' they laid him on the grass - where he died.   Eight men were arrested.   It took three days trying to sort out the case because it was necessary to wait until they were sufficiently sober.   The police spent 98 hours on the initial investigations, including 20 hours spent enquiring of secondhand dealers about the watch stolen from the deceased. Sixty hours were spent on interviewing, investigating the suspects' backgrounds (50 hours), and a further 20 hours preparing case papers.   Four men were released

and 4 charged with robbery. The Director of Public Prosecutions later directed that an additional charge of administering a noxious drug be added to the indictment. After their trial 3 men were found not guilty and the fourth was sentenced to 12 months imprisonment on the one charge and an additional 3 months on the second.

94. Derek A., 19 years, is an outpatient registered at a psychiatric hospital. He alleged that at 2345 one night he was attacked in the street and robbed of £3 and a pair of shoes (described as 'black brothel creepers'). The story he gave of his movements that evening aroused suspicion because he said he had taken 1 hour 10 minutes to get from one place to another but only 10 minutes to cover a comparable distance later. Interviewed the following day he said that on the previous evening he had taken his pills for epilepsy, drunk 6 or 7 pints of beer during the day and another 5 or 6 during the evening. He said that this left him 'really canned'. Later he had found the missing shoes in the street. He also said that as he left home with only £2 he could not have been robbed of a greater sum. His injuries were compatible with a fall or an assault. He made a further statement withdrawing the complaint. The police spent 2 hours on the case. The complainant in this case was subsequently convicted for the offence of theft described in Chapter Two as case no. 144.

ROBBERIES IN TAXIS

2. Maureen F., 31 years, had a row with her husband, who beat her. She came into town, got drunk, and booked into a hotel. She gave a taxi driver £20 to fetch her a bottle of Scotch. Later, three taxi-drivers came to her hotel. She bought them breakfast and hired two of them to drive her home. In the taxi she was robbed of £970 in cash and a £30 bracelet and then pushed out on to the road. She flagged down a motorist who brought her to the police station at 1100 hours.

The victim remembered the taxi drivers' call number and the firm was identified. On arrest, one man named two others. Arrested, the second man asserted that he threw his £50 into the river. The police called at the residence of the third, to be told that he was not at home. The suspect tried to escape over the roof and was caught. £400 was recovered from the house. The third suspect was incensed that the police should not have believed his sister when she alleged that he was not in the house. His mother, who could not speak English, was brought to the police station to help identify which of the seized bank notes were the proceeds of the robbery. She vehemently asserted that the British people were rubbish.

One of the accused (Mohammed) told his employers that he had been charged with an offence; they kept him on and his girlfriend stood by him. He pleaded guilty in the Crown Court and insisted on testifying as a prosecution witness against the other man (Mahar), who pleaded not guilty - apparently to defend family honour. Mohammed was sentenced to 6 months imprisonment suspended for 2 years and ordered to pay £450 compensation. Mahar was found guilty; he was sentenced to 6 months for robbery and a further 3 months for two separate offences of driving while disqualified and being in breach of a Community Service Order and a conditional discharge. Later in the year he admitted to his solicitor that he had been responsible for the crime. The police gave the report a screening score of 20; they spent $24\frac{1}{2}$ hours on the initial investigation and 23 hours interviewing the suspects and enquiring into their backgrounds.

90. Adam C., is a taxi driver who was hired in Exeter by two men who later held a knife to his throat and obliged him to drive to Bristol. En route he was robbed of various documents including money and a bank card. In Bristol they forced him, again at knife point, to use the card to withdraw money from a cash dispenser. He alleged that he had already drawn out £40 that day so that he would be able to get only £10. The men believed him. After he had withdrawn the money they grabbed it and ran off. The taxi driver reported the offence to the police, who were initially sceptical. Then they made enquiries at a taxi rank and found a driver who had been hired by two men answering the description to drive them to a hotel. Enquiring there, the police learned that the hotelier had directed them to a restaurant. At the restaurant the offenders were arrested. The police gave the report a score of 32; they spent 32 hours on the initial enquiry (12 of them at the Exeter end), and 10 hours arresting and interviewing the suspects, 14 hours preparing case papers, and four hours in the magistrates' court. In the Crown Court they pleaded

not guilty to charges of kidnapping and guilty to robbery. The former charges were not proceeded with. On the latter each offender was sentenced to 7 years imprisonment and ordered to make payments of restitution to the taxi driver.

5 Detection

From the review of case histories it will be apparent that reports of robbery vary greatly in their seriousness and investigability. Many of the more serious offences were detected. It should be possible to assess the success of police enquiries by comparing the outcomes with the initial scoring of the reports by the Detective Inspector as described in Chapter One.

The method of scoring used was one based upon a model developed by the Stanford Research Institute in California (see Appendix 4). It was modified by the detective inspector and detective superintendent in Bristol to reflect their method of assessing reports. My view was that any points system had to be as factual as possible, keeping to a minimum the opportunity for variations stemming from personal judgements. I acknowledged that this would fail to measure some relevant features of reports but hoped that at least it would be reliable in the sense that practically anyone evaluating a report would give it a similar score. The police, however, wanted something more flexible that would reflect such variables as public concern. In the event the screening scores did not work very well. On a number of occasions reports were, by accident, screened twice, and the scores differed, sometimes significantly. I have therefore had to examine them and check such variations. The experience shows that it would have been better to work with two separate scores, the first being designed to measure the chances of successful detection and the second to reflect the seriousness with which the alleged events were viewed. In my analysis I have therefore extracted two scores. The first, called solvability, is the sum of the scores given on form C (Appendix 3) to the information about the offender, including movement description and physical evidence. The second is the seriousness score based upon the remaining items.

Table 18
The results of investigation

	Solvability Scores				Seriousness Scores			
	dubious	undetected	suspect	detected	dubious	undetected	suspect	detected
Street Robberies								
0-3	18	46	2	4	18	42	2	10
4-7	5	15	2	5	6	17	1	2
8-11	2	2	1	3	1	2	1	2
12-	-	-	-	3	-	2	1	1
Shops and Houses								
0-3	-	5	-	4	-	3	-	5
4-7	-	2	-	5	-	-	-	3
8 -11	-	-	1	2	-	3	-	3
12-	-	-	-	4	-	1	1	4
Other Robberies								
0-3	5	6	-	4	4	5	-	4
4-7	1	1	-	-	3	1	-	5
8-11	-	-	-	-	-	1	-	1
12-	1	-	-	8	-	-	-	2

Note: Cases which resulted in a prosecution for robbery or related offence have been counted as detected whether or not the prosecution succeeded. A prosecution of an offender for the sale of the proceeds of a robbery has not been counted as related or as a detection. Three street robberies reclassified as 'no crime' have been included with the dubious reports.

From Table 18 it can be seen that more than two-thirds of the street robberies fell in the lowest category with respect to both solvability and seriousness. The police were slightly more successful in detecting the cases with higher solvability scores. This relationship, however, is much stronger with respect to robberies in shops and houses, and 'other robberies'. Robberies in shops and houses are in general regarded as the most serious, and it is here that detection rates are highest, particularly in the detection of armed robberies where 5 cases resulted in 3 detections and a fourth case in which it seems certain that the culprit was a man convicted of one of the other armed robberies. This points to the unsurprising conclusion that the official figures of percentage of crimes detected underestimates the true success of police investigations.

To consider whether the police might be more successful had they greater resources, it is of interest to examine the seven cases which were given solvability scores of eight or more but which remained undetected. Five of these were street robberies, two of which were classed as dubious complaints (142 in which the aggrieved gave a false address and disappeared; it seemed to be one in a sequence of disputes between two parties well known to one another; 48, reported by the old lady who seems to have had a fall coming back from the pub). In one case (148) the detectives were confident they had the right men but although they had spent just over 50 hours on the case they could not assemble sufficient evidence and charges had been refused. The fourth related to Maurice C. described as a 'professional victim' and to the incident (39) in which he was robbed by someone who wanted to buy fish and chips. The fifth (143) concerned the theft of £800 being part of a sum obtained by deception in which it was impossible to establish with confidence what had happened. The sixth (15), was a Post Office robbery in which 107 hours had been spent on the enquiry and the prime suspect had been convicted of a similar offence. The last of the seven (37) was the one described as 'a drinking party that went wrong' and recorded as 'no crime'. If these were the cases that appeared solvable but did not result in detection, this would not suggest that an increase in police resources would produce many more detections for robbery.

ETHNICITY

A very high proportion of all the robberies in the area studied were carried out by young black males. As can be seen from Table 18, it is possible that twice as many street robberies were carried out by blacks as by whites. However,

Table 19
Table 19
Ethnicity of victim and offender, street robberies

	Offender: White	Asian	Black	Mixed Group
Male victim				
White				
independent evidence	5	–	7	–
no independent evidence	13	–	26	1
dubious complaint	2	1	14	2
Asian				
independent evidence	–	–	–	–
no independent evidence	–	–	1	–
dubious complaint	–	–	2	–
Black				
independent evidence	–	–	1	–
no independent evidence	–	–	1	–
dubious complaint	–	–	1	–
Female victim				
White				
independent evidence	1	–	2	–
no independent evidence	2	–	2	1
dubious complaint	–	–	–	1
Known carrier of cash				
White				
male and female	3	–	11	–

Notes: A dubious complaint is one so described in the text of chapters Two to Four together with reports reclassified as 'no crime'.   Two cases have been excluded from the figures relating to male victims for lack of evidence as to the ethnic identity of the offender.   In the second line of those relating to female victims the figure in the last column was not a group but a single female alleged offender described by the victim as 'half caste'.   One case has been excluded from the figures relating to known carriers of cash for lack of evidence about the ethnic identity of the offender.

Table 20
Ethnicity of victim and offender, other robberies

Victim	Offender:	White	Asian	Black	Mixed Group
Robberies in shops and houses, unarmed					
White		7	-	6	1
Asian		1	-	3	-
Robberies in shops and houses, armed					
White		2	-	3	-
Robberies connected with prostitution					
White		3	-	6	4
dubious complaint		-	-	1	-
Robberies connected with drugs and drink					
White		5	-	2	-
dubious complaint		-	-	2	-
Robberies in taxis					
White		1	1	-	-

Table 21
Ethnicity of victim and offender, white complainants

	Offender:	White	Asian	Black	Mixed Group
Street robberies					
independent evidence		6	-	9	-
no independent evidence		15	-	28	1
dubious complaint		1	1	14	3
Other robberies		21	-	30	5
Dubious complaint		-	-	3	-

82

it is necessary to interpret Table 18 with great caution because of the small numbers involved. As was mentioned in Chapter One, the total number of robberies per annum in Bristol over the period 1975-83 has varied significantly from year to year, suggesting that the incidence of this offence may be greatly affected by the activities of small numbers of young men. If any attempt were to be made to assess the relative participation of black and white offenders in the committing of any particular offence or offences, the research worker would have first to allow for the effect upon the figures of the activity of some men in committing multiple offences. The research worker would next have to control for the influence of relevant variables in the social background, like income, employment, family stability, and so on, to make sure that he or she was comparing like with like. If attention was paid to some particular offence, it would be necessary to see whether the offending was part of a more general pattern. No such analysis is attempted here, and the figures are best seen simply for the light they cast on problems as they confront the police.

From this limited perspective, two features can be mentioned. The first is that many of the white victims, when asked to describe the man who robbed them, had difficulty giving good descriptions. Older white people in particular might describe an offender as coloured but say that they would be unable to identify him if they were to attend a parade. For many of them 'all coloured people look the same'. If this is the case, then it increases the chances that black youths may be able to commit such offences without detection. A second feature is that since black youths are believed to specialize in this sort of offence, white people who allege that they have been robbed in order to account for their having lost or spent their money, are more likely to describe their robbers as coloured. As can be seen from Table 18, the proportion of white male victims who said that the robber was coloured or black was higher when there was no independent evidence that any robbery occurred, and when the complaint was regarded as dubious by the police 15 times out of 16 the robber was said to be coloured. (At the time in question the general tendency in Bristol was for whites to describe all people of New Commonwealth origin as coloured, and to differentiate between South Asians and Blacks only when asked for more detail.) Table 20 summarizes all the reports of robbery made by whites in which any information was provided about the ethnic identity of the alleged offender. If the ratio of black to white offenders in cases in which there was independent evidence were repeated in the second line of the table, the figure for black offenders would be 22 or 23 not 28. The difference is not great, but the big difference in

83

the line for dubious complaints supports the inference that in some of the alleged robberies by blacks in which there was no independent evidence there was in reality no robbery committed.

The detectives also found that when investigating an offence allegedly committed by a black offender they received less cooperation from the residents of the area than in comparable circumstances they would have received from white residents. Much might depend upon the nature of the offence and whether the offender was someone likely to threaten anyone testifying against him. One detective commented that he and his colleagues had received a lot of help from the black community in tracking down a black rapist: 'the blacks told us whom to arrest but they won't testify in court'. At that time they had in the cells a man whom they believed had buggered a prostitute while she was drunk; then, realizing that a semen test might lead to his identification, he burned the woman round the anus with a cigarette lighter to remove any traces. He also burned her underclothing. She had been found running round the streets naked. Though initially she had been willing to talk about what had happened, she had become frightened. The police asked 'Can we ask a court to remand him in custody for perhaps eight weeks when we know that at the end of it all there is a distinct possibility that she will decline to testify?'

Another detective who had worked on this sub-division for some years prior to 1976, and had recently returned to it after six years elsewhere, expressed the opinion that over this period the style of policing had become softer with the result that suspects were now less willing to talk to the police. 'If we can talk to people we are half way there' he said. When interviewing suspects he usually discussed other matters for the first quarter of an hour in order to establish a relationship with the interviewee. In the past when youths, black or white, left the cells, they usually regarded the detectives as friends. There were fewer interventions from solicitors then. Solicitors now (he said) are under more pressure from their clients' families and they try harder to get them off. 'If you could take away thirty to forty black men you could remove most of the crime in St. Paul's. Nowadays the black youths just won't talk, even, like in one case we had recently, when they've been caught coming out of a house with a holdall containing stolen goods. Even sixteen-year olds aren't talking'. This detective was quite sure that policing in the sub-division had become more difficult. The increase in criminality would suggest that more people in the locality were suffering more frequently from the depredations of other residents and that this had increased the tension between victims, witnesses, offenders, and police.

The special features of this locality create difficulties for any comparison with robbery statistics for larger districts, but it seems probable that they fit into an overall pattern. Crime statistics for the Metropolitan Police District, 1977-83, suggest that a disproportionately large number of Asians were victims of robbery, compared with members of other ethnic groups. In 1983, 10 per cent of the London victims were recorded as being of Indian/Pakistani/ Bangladeshi appearance, whereas such minorities constituted 4 per cent of the total population. In Bristol also, Asians may be victimized disproportionately often, but, if so, the figures do not yet establish this. In London, judging from victims' descriptions of their attackers, a disproportionately large number of non-whites were responsible for street robberies and 'snatches' (58 per cent of 1983 offenders being described as non-white whereas non-whites constitute 9 per cent of the total population). Because over 70 per cent of these offences are committed by young men under 21 years of age, it is better to compare the crime figure with that showing 21 per cent of the population aged 10-20 years to be non-white (9 per cent of West Indian/African origin, 12 per cent of Asian origin). A further complication arises because the crime figures aggregate blacks and Asians. Since relatively few of the latter commit robberies, and proportionately more are victims, there are additional grounds for believing that in London street robberies and bag-snatching (which may involve little threat of violence) are perpetrated disproportionately often by young blacks. It does not appear as if young blacks in Bristol are involved in this offence anywhere near as often as those in London.

Any analysis indicating that members of a particular ethnic group are disproportionately responsible for a certain kind of crime arouses apprehension because it reinforces tendencies to stereotyping. If the figures suggest that a higher proportion of some crime is committed by blacks than by whites, people easily overlook the indication that the percentages of both blacks and whites involved in that crime are relatively small; they may treat any black man as a potential risk when he has done nothing whatsoever to justify such suspicion. This poses a serious educational and political problem. Steps need to be taken continually to counteract the tendencies to stereotyping but they will not be assisted by the suppression of the statistics about alleged offenders which are routinely collected when crimes are recorded.

SENTENCES

Following through the case studies, it will have been noticed that when offenders were brought to trial it was sometimes on lesser charges. In the end, therefore, 16 adult males were convicted of robbery, 2 of aggravated burglary and 1 of theft; 10 young adult males (i.e., aged 17-20 years) were convicted of robbery, 2 on the reduced charges of assault causing grievous bodily harm together with theft, and 3 on the reduced charge of theft. For robbery, 2 young adult females were also convicted. Among juvenile males, 3 were convicted of robbery and 1 of assault with intent to rob. The sentences are set out below, in declining order of seriousness.

Case 121. For murder and robbery, Milton H., 24 years, was sentenced to life imprisonment; he had 12 previous convictions for burglary and theft and had previously been sentenced to imprisonment (4 times), Borstal, detention centre and community service. His accomplice, Andrew D., 21 years, who had 3 previous convictions for burglary, assault, and abusive behaviour, was made subject to a community service order.

Case 45 was the armed hold-up in the bank. Convicted of attempted murder and robbery, Donovan R., 28 years, was sentenced to life imprisonment. He had 12 previous convictions, starting with burglary at age 15, theft, and then possession of an offensive weapon (knife) in a public place, (for which he was committed to a detention centre), followed by repeated offences of theft, burglary, assault and taking a motor vehicle, for which he had twice been sent to Borstal and 5 times to prison. Shortly after release from his last sentence he had been charged with unlawful possession of a sawn-off shot gun; allowed bail, he failed to attend for trial, and was wanted on warrant. His young adult accomplice who after the bank robbery hi-jacked the lorry, had one previous conviction (for grievous bodily harm) as a juvenile. He too was sentenced to life imprisonment.

While serving these sentences, Donovan R. and Sebastian K. were prosecuted and convicted for 37 other offences connected with the attempted bank robbery in Bristol and a series of earlier bank robberies in London. One of the latter was an armed robbery in which a policeman and a security guard were shot and a gun discharged at a member of the public who chased them in his car. Sentences for these further offences included two more sentences of life imprisonment for each offender.

Case 145 was the attempted armed robbery of the Post Office van for which Arthur S., 21 years, with one previous conviction for theft, was sentenced to 7 years; Reginald D., with previous convictions for burglary, to 6 years; and Luke S., with seventeen previous convictions for burglary, theft and assault, to 4 years imprisonment.

Case 90 was the robbery and kidnapping of the taxi driver as a result of which Harold J., 25 years, and Richard K., 41 years, were each imprisoned for 7 years for robbery. On appeal, Harold's sentence was reduced to one of 5 year's imprisonment.

Richard had been convicted on 18 previous occasions, for theft, burglary, taking motor vehicles, assaulting a police oficer and, on three occasions, for unlawful wounding. He had been placed on probation 5 times, served a period of Borstal training and 10 times been imprisoned, twice for a sentence of two years.

Harold had been convicted on 24 previous occasions, mostly for theft and burglary but also for assault and assault on a police officer. He too had been sentenced to Borstal training and had been placed on probation; he had been bound over, conditionally discharged, fined and sentenced to imprisonment on twelve occasions (on three of them the sentence had been suspended). The longest sentences had been for three years and three years three months.

Cases 10 and 41 were the robberies of the filling station and the fur shop for which Donald R. and his young adult accomplice Alan Y. were convicted (see also cases 15 and 18). Donald had been convicted previously on 16 occasions for robbery, burglary, theft, assault, etc.; he was sentenced to a total of 4 years imprisonment for one robbery and two thefts, plus a further 2 months in respect of a suspended sentence. He subsequently appealed (see Chapter Six). Alan, who was on licence from Borstal, was sentenced to 3½ years youth custody. He had previously been convicted for assault with intent to rob, including the possession of a weapon.

Case 57A, was the aggravated burglary; Henry B., 22 years, and Kevin C., 32 years, were each sentenced to

4 years imprisonment.   Henry had a record of 12 previous offences of burglary, theft and taking a motor vehicle; Kevin's record was less serious.

Case 97, for robbery of the elderly man in his house, Max J., 40 years, with 10 previous convictions, was imprisoned for 2 years, and his accomplice, Howard S., 25 years, with a record of 8 previous convictions, for 15 months.

Case 21, for the robbery of 3 filling stations, the 35-year-old   Matthew F., a man with five previous convictions for burglary and theft, was sentenced to 3 years imprisonment.

Case 8, for the robbery of the mail bag, Alfred J., 22 years, was sent to prison for 2 years.

Case 83, for robbery and administering a noxious drug (the case in which the alcoholic died), a 44 year old man called Patrick K. was imprisoned for 15 months. He had been convicted 39 times previously, for burglary, theft, receiving stolen property, forgery, assault, and gross indecency.

Case 43, for robbery of a filling station, Kenneth S., a man of 38 years with 30 previous convictions, mostly for burglary, was imprisoned for 15 months.

Case 2, was that in which two men robbed a woman in a taxi.   Maher, the one who pleaded not guilty, was, after conviction, sentenced to 6 months imprisonment; Mohammed, who admitted the offence, was sentenced to 6 months, suspended for 2 years.   Maher was also convicted of driving while disqualified; his sentence of 6 months imprisonment for this offence was to run concurrently with the other sentence.

Cases 113, 115, 117, 118 and 119, in which a group of young men and two young women robbed men who came to a house for prostitution, resulted in 4 convictions. Two brothers named Norman and Roger T., one 18 years and the other 17 years, were sentenced to 3 years and 1 year's youth custody;   the 18-year-old woman was ordered to perform 180 hours community service while the younger woman was eventually placed on probation for two years.

Case 71, for robbing a filling station, Roberto B., 20 years, was sentenced to 3 years youth custody; he had

9 previous convictions, for burglary, theft, assault and taking away a motor vehicle.

Case 146, for a street robbery, a 20-year-old man named David D., with 3 previous convictions for robbery, burglary and threatening behaviour, was sentenced to 2 years and 3 months youth custody. His 18-year-old co-accused, Edward S., who had 3' previous convictions for burglary, theft, taking a vehicle and driving with excess alcohol, was sentenced to 15 months in youth custody.

Case 159, a street robbery, resulted in 15 months youth custody for Albert A., 19 years, a young man with 8 previous convictions, mostly for burglary and theft.

Case 77, another street robbery in which the 17-year-old accused, Eric M., was also convicted of unlawful and malicious wounding, led to a sentence of 9 months youth custody.

Case 116, in which two 20-year-old youths, Jimmie M. and Sidney T., attempted to steal a bottle of brandy, brought a sentence of 9 months youth custody for the former and 3 years probation for the latter. Jimmie had six previous convictions for robbery, burglary, theft, and taking a motor vehicle. Sidney had also been convicted six times before, for theft and receiving stolen property.

Case 123, a street robbery, resulted in a 19-year-old male, who had 6 previous convictions for burglary, theft, and motoring offences, being ordered to perform 200 hours community service.

Case 33, was one in which the charge was reduced to that of theft, but a 19-year-old man was also convicted of two offences of burglary. He had previously been convicted on three occasions of theft and twice of assault. He was sentenced to 2 years youth custody.

Case 144, was one in which the accused was willing to admit to a charge of theft. Derek A., 20 years, had 6 previous convictions for theft, criminal damage and drunkenness. He was placed on probation for one year.

Case 19, in which a 19-year-old youth, Clive R., who had recently completed a prison sentence, was convicted for an earlier robbery of a shop, was dealt with by a conditional discharge.

Case 40 involved two juveniles, Trevor G., aged 16, and Lance H., aged 15 years. Trevor, who was also convicted for the unlawful possession of a drug, was sentenced to 12 months youth custody; Lance, who had a previous conviction for burglary, was sentenced to 6 months youth custody.

Case 140, a street robbery, concerned a juvenile with no previous convictions. He was convicted on this occasion of robbery, blackmail, theft, and criminal damage, made subject to a supervision order for 2 years, and ordered to pay £150 costs.

Case 68, a street robbery, led to the prosecution of a 16-year-old male, for assault with intent to rob. He had two previous convictions for theft and criminal damage. He was fined £50.

Perhaps the most striking feature of this list is the high proportion of cases in which the offenders had been previously convicted. Many of them show the pattern of a criminal career in which the offender is convicted for progressively more serious offences and made subject to increasingly severe sentences. It is also possible that once someone has been convicted of an offence he or she is more likely to become a suspect when new offences are reported. The police officers know the records of the people with whom they have to deal and inevitably this influences their estimate of the suspects' moral deserts.

6 Conclusion

The starting point for this study was a question put to me about the adequacy of police powers for investigating serious crime. Nothing that I have learned in conducting the research has led me to believe that the police could do much to reduce the incidence of robbery. Banks, post offices, filling stations and persons who have to carry cash or valuables from one point to another have all become much more security conscious over the last twenty years without being able to reduce the frequency of attempted robbery. Members of the public walking the streets, especially at night and in the city centres, are more vulnerable, but they value their liberty too much to stay indoors, even if a substantial number of older people are afraid to go out.

But if the increase in robbery reflects the circumstances of modern urban living, it might still be possible to improve the effectiveness of the police in apprehending the offenders. A simple increase in police strength would have little effect, to judge from a Home Office study (Burrows and Tarling 1982, pp. 11-12) which concluded that a one per cent increase in the number of police officers, devoted solely to increasing the time spent on crime detection by the CID, would produce a less than one per cent increase in the clear-up rate. The major obstacle to improved effectiveness is that of identification. This study has demonstrated how diverse are the incidents which are subsequently classified as robberies; any

91

conjectures about the causes for the increase in this particular kind of crime must allow for that. It has shown that several times one individual has been responsible for a series of robberies while the similarity of descriptions, places, and times suggests that particular groups of youths who were not identified in 1983 may have been responsible for multiple offences. The variations in annual totals (between 119 and 313 in a seven-year period) support the view that when the more persistent offenders are imprisoned, the incidence drops. If the apparent success of such offenders suggests that the risks are low, others may follow suit. Yet identification, even of the persistent offenders, is difficult. Few victims are able to name the person who has robbed them. Few can describe the robber in such a way as to make identification easy. A significant proportion of persons reporting that they have been robbed say at the same time that they do not believe they could recognize the person responsible. Some are not willing even to try. The more serious robberies usually attract more attention, and are doubtless talked about, which makes the detectives' task a little easier, but in some of these cases witnesses who could identify an offender are afraid to do so and police powers to protect witnesses are limited.

IDENTITY PARADES

Other issues are raised concerning the adequacy of police powers in the conduct of identity parades. An interesting example was provided by a robbery which occurred on the subdivision just after the research period terminated.

> 161. On 18th January 1984 at 0925 two female members of staff were in Bannerman Road Post Office when two men entered. One bought chewing gum. Just then a Post Office van drew up outside to make a delivery. The first of two postmen in the van came out, looked around, and signalled to the second that he could leave the van and take the delivery box into the Post Office. He did this while the first man stood guard. In the office the second postman was attacked by the two men already there, one of them hitting him with a piece of wood. But fairly soon the two attackers ran off without the delivery box. In the road one of them hesitated as if he were thinking of going back to try again to get it. He seemed more than usually determined. By this time several alarms were sounding and, seeing signs of pursuit, the two robbers ran off, got into a car round the corner, and drove away at speed. The police reached the Post Office within 5

minutes.   Within 10 minutes they had identified the
vehicle as registered in the name of a man living in
Knowle.   Police records showed that his son had a
criminal record.   The vehicle was thought to be used
by the owner's brother, Joseph B.   Twenty-five minutes
after the robbery the vehicle was located, empty, a
short distance from Joseph's house.   The police called
at the house and, finding a rear door insecure,
entered and waited.   After a further fifteen minutes
Joseph returned in a track suit and running shoes.   He
said he has been out jogging since 0930 but the police
suspected him of being one of the robbers, so they
arrested him.

After a further 5 minutes, George L. came to the
house.   Since he fitted the description of the other
robber, he was arrested.   Four years earlier George
had been arrested in connection with the robbery of a
nearby Post Office in which a postman had been hit on
the head with a wooden stick and £7,000 stolen.
George's finger prints had been found on a bag wrapped
around the offensive weapon and upon another bag
behind the counter into which the robbers had been
putting money.   He and another man who admitted
participation had been arrested.   When, seven months
later, they were before the court, only the other man
had been committed for trial.   The evidence against
George was adjudged insufficient since the prosecution
were unable to prove that George's fingerprints could
not have come onto the bags legitimately.   The other
man, although a first offender, was imprisoned for
five years; at first he had named George as an
accomplice but later withdrew this.   The police knew
of six other post office robberies in the region which
had been carried out in a similar manner;   they had
their suspicions of George but he refused to take part
in any identity parade.

Three years earlier in Bristol George had grabbed a
Post Office bag and run off with it.   A taxi driver
picked up the postman and they pursued him.   The bag,
containing £37,000, was found.   A former associate of
George's, who hated him, had helped identify him and,
when arrested, George had admitted the offence; for it
he was sentenced to two and a half years'
imprisonment.   This record indicated that George was
no stranger to the sort of offence under investigation
and strengthened the grounds for suspicion.

There were seven witnesses to the Bannerman Road

robbery.   There were grounds to believe that about
0830 that morning Joseph had driven his girl friend to
hospital but he was unwilling to admit this, alleging
that his car was missing.   Later his solicitor told
the police that Joseph would admit the offence but
would neither implicate George nor testify against
him.   Joseph seemed to be frightened of George.   The
police view of the matter was that since an elderly
postman had been quite viciously assaulted (even if
only by his companion) Joseph might fear a severe
sentence and therefore be inclined to confess in order
to reduce that sentence.   The police thought that
Joseph was a 'pudden', a thick-headed man; they found
it difficult to 'get through to him'.   One detective
thought that he was under someone else's influence
since he was so sure that the police were trying to
trick him.   They had a statement from another witness
who described Joseph as a dreamer who had talked of
doing 'a big Post Office job'.   This witness had been
concerned about Joseph for fear that he would do
something stupid.

Identification of the second and more determined
robber was less easy.   Of the seven witnesses, four
said he was clean shaven; one said he had a beard, and
two were doubtful.   When first interviewed George was
ready to talk about his family, his acquaintances, his
experience of prison, and so on, but denied
participation in the robbery.   When re-interviewed he
simply lay on his back and refused to say more than
that 'You've got to release me in 48 hours'.   Then he
said he would go on an identity parade.   When told
that there were seven witnesses he wanted to know what
would happen if only one of the seven identified him.
It was suggested that in such circumstances he might
be bailed.   He replied that he did not wish to be
bailed; he would sit it out.   He did not want a
solicitor.   Since George is a black man the police
invited a black solicitor's clerk to come and see him
as they feared their case might be weakened were it
alleged in court that they had frustrated the
suspect's desire to consult a solicitor.   The clerk in
question had difficulty persuading George that he was
not a policeman in disguise but after two hours George
completed a 'green form' applying for legal aid.   Then
attempts were made to arrange an identity parade.
Witnesses attended for 1900 hours.   George
prevaricated.   At 2030 he finally refused to take
part.   In the police view the Home Office rules
concerning identity parades implied that when a

suspect was unwilling to take part the suspect should be placed in a group to see if a witness could identify him in those circumstances.

At 1330 on the third day the witnesses attended again. George was carried out of his cell by four police officers, one holding each corner of his mattress. Other young black men had agreed to attend the parade, to be handcuffed like George, and to behave just like George so that if he screamed, they would scream, and if he threw himself about, so would they. So the witnesses saw a row of young men, handcuffed, sitting on chairs; each one with a uniformed policeman behind him and identified by placards bearing the letters A to L. Solicitors for the accused agreed to attend while stipulating that their presence did not imply approval of the procedure followed. This parade or group identification was recorded on video and George behaved normally. As three of the seven witnesses identified George he was charged with robbery and taken to court before the 72 hours allowed for detention had expired.

The police had consulted the Director of Public Prosecutions before adopting this procedure. They did not know what else to do in the circumstances but had many questions about the whole situation. Had they gone too far? Would the judge say that had parliament intended to permit forcible identity parades they would have provided for them? Would it not be better if the police could apply to a court for permission to conduct a parade just as they could seek orders for finger printing? The Home Office rules allowed them to pay £3 to volunteers who would make up an identity parade but this was not always sufficient, especially in circumstances such as those of the parade just arranged. Witnesses were supposed to touch any person they identified but this inhibits some witnesses. The parade for George had been arranged just after a change of shift, constables on the early turn being required to stay on. They had needed twenty-five police officers for the parade and a total of over 31 hours of police time quite apart from the time of the detectives and the inspector. Without holding such a parade they could not have been sure that George had been one of the robbers.

On 1st March George was granted bail by a judge sitting in chambers. He said that in his opinion the identity parade had not been legal.

95

In the normal course of events the police record the
names and addresses of members of the public who make
up a parade on a form which is used to account for the
£3 each has been paid for participating. (Since the
police in this subdivision have great difficulty
obtaining volunteers similar in appearance to black
suspects they have been authorized to pay £5 when
necessary.) Copies of this form are not given to the
defence unless the judge so instructs. When the case
came to trial the judge instructed the prosecution to
supply this form, with the result that the evidence
was stopped on various occasions while defence called
participants in the parade, as they became available;
they were placed in the dock beside the defendant so
the jury could see if they were sufficiently similar.
At the trial, counsel for the defence objected that
the identification evidence was inadmissible. She
submitted that this was to all intents and purposes an
identification parade and that therefore the police
should be bound by its rules. She maintained that
there had been many breaches of these rules,
including: breach of rule 14 in that the other
coloured men in the line were not of the same age,
height, or personal appearance as the accused,
especially in that only one had any sort of beard, and
only two others were wearing indoor clothes like the
accused; breach of rule 17, in that the identification
witnesses were brought in together instead of singly;
breach of rule 20, as no witness either touched or
pointed out the person identified. If the court did
not accept that this was a parade then it must have
been a group identification. In that case, according
to the defence counsel, there had been a breach of
paragraph 5 of the Administrative Guidance in Home
Office Circular 109/78 which implied that each witness
should separately see the suspects as one person in a
group. The circumstances in which the identification
took place were so unfair that its probative value was
minimal and the court should not allow it to be
introduced.

The judge agreed with the prosecution submission that
once an accused person had refused to take part in an
identity parade he had to accept that the procedure
followed might be less satisfactory. 'He is entitled
to refuse but he has to accept the consequences . . .
In this case I do not think that there is any trickery
by the police . . . In my view the confrontation –
for that is what I find it was, as the accused had
refused an identification parade – is not to be

treated as an identification parade . . . I appreciate fully the problems of the police, and I realize their anxiety that the accused might create a disturbance to draw attention to himself, and if so that might bring the strength of any identification into question, but that could happen if all the witnesses were there together, and in my view the police should have brought each witness in separately . . . In my view the police here were trying to be fair to be accused. In certain respects in fact I think they adopted a wrong procedure, not only in letting the witnesses view en bloc, as I have already stated, but also in not after this when they had identified the accused and marked their form, in not asking each who had made an identification to point to the person they identified, as there is a risk – one can put it no higher than that – that the witness in error might have marked the letter of the person they had not in fact identified'. He allowed the evidence, and, when summing up at the end of the trial, drew to the jury's attention the respects in which the procedure of the police had weakened their case. The accused was acquitted. Had he been convicted, the defence would probably have appealed and the legality of the police action could then have been settled by the Appeal Court. Since the prosecution cannot now appeal they have been unable to get this matter settled.

In conclusion, it may be noted that the Post Office delivery box which was the object of the attempted robbery contained just £11.50 worth of air mail envelopes.

The difficulties which the police can experience in meeting the current legal criteria for the identification of persons to be prosecuted are also illustrated by cases 10 and 41 in which Donald R. was accused of robbing a filling station and a shop that sold furs. One Thursday an identity parade was arranged which involved sixteen persons described in court as coloured men. The manageress of the shop, Mrs. Pauline P., was brought in to see if she identified Donald and Alan Y. who were among the sixteen. Remembering that the robber who had threatened her with a knife had said 'I have been drinking. I don't care', Pauline asked the inspector in charge of the parade if the men could be asked to say something so that she could see if she recognized a voice as well. The inspector made a note of this request upon his clipboard, whereupon the solicitor representing Alan objected that while the inspector did this it would have been possible for Pauline to see marks on a paper on the inspector's clipboard which would have indicated to her the positions which Donald and Alan occupied on the parade. Pauline said she had not seen this, but she was taken out of the room. She noticed Alan on her way out and identified him. The shop assistant, Miss Anne M., next entered and identified Alan but not Donald. On the following Sunday afternoon, three days later, Pauline was invited to attend the police station where she was shown a coloured man sitting in a room with someone she understood to be his solicitor. She confidently identified this man as the taller of the two robbers who had entered her shop.

At the trial, defence counsel objected to the admissibility of Pauline's evidence concerning the identification on the Sunday, so, before she reached this part of her testimony, the judge instructed the jury to retire while he listened to the argument about admissibility. The defence referred to Home Office Circular 109/78 (mentioned in the previous case) according to which:

'If a suspect refuses to attend a parade, arrangements may be made to allow the witness an opportunity of seeing him in a group of people to test the witness's ability to identify the person whom he said he saw on a previous occasion. Care should be taken not to draw the witness's attention to the suspect.

A suspect should only be confronted by a witness if it is impracticable to arrange for any alternative method of identification in a group situation, e.g. in the case of a suspect of singular appearance.'

The position was that Donald had agreed to go on an identity parade before Pauline. That parade had gone wrong on technical grounds and had been cancelled. Donald was unwilling to take part in a second parade. The police should therefore have arranged for Pauline to see him as one of a group and only if that had been impracticable should they have arranged for confrontation between the two parties to see if Pauline identified Donald. Since they had not arranged a group identification, then, according to the defence, the evidence arising from the confrontation should not be admitted.

The prosecution contested this. The detectives testified that, hearing of the failure of the identity parade, they had reinterviewed Donald on the Friday and the Saturday and on both occasions he had declined to take part in a further parade. They said that it had been difficult to get twelve volunteers similar to Donald for the first parade. They could not go back to the same volunteers. As one said, 'If you try to round up large numbers to assist you from the streets of St. Pauls, you are greeted with great suspicion. You have great difficulty getting a West Indian youth to come to the station which is one and a half miles away'. Time was running out for them because the accused was due back in court on the Monday. Other policemen testified about the parade and Pauline spoke about her identification. The judge ruled that her testimony was admissible. He said

'I have to consider whether it was in fact impracticable for the officers to arrange a group of young coloured males in which to put this defendant . . . The matter did not arise unfortunately, until late on a Saturday night, because by chance the defendant's Solicitor was involved in moving house. Therefore any group would have had to be organized by the Police at a time when the shops and public houses, including the amusement arcades, had shut. It is on the evidence I have heard, difficult enough to collect a number of similar people to stand on an identification parade on a weekday, because of the underlying suspicion among the black community when any member of their community is asked to attend at the police station for whatever purpose . . . I find that the police were right in their decision that it was not practicable to attempt to get together a group of blacks for a group identification, and that they therefore did not comply with the administrative guidance . . . In any event, I find that . . . in the circumstances of this case it would be wrong to exclude the evidence; because the witness, it seems to me, is a credible witness on the face of her evidence. I think that if the Jury is properly warned of the distinctions between an identification parade and a confrontation, no injustice will be done to the defendant. Indeed, it is almost too obvious to point out how much less weight a confrontation has by way of evidence than an identification parade'.

The trial continued on that basis. Giving evidence on his own behalf, Donald stated that on the day in question he had been out with his wife; they returned home at 3.20 or 3.30 p.m. (the robbery having occurred about 3.30-3.45 p.m.). His wife and her sister supported this alibi. The jury nevertheless found him guilty. After conviction, Donald pleaded guilty to two charges of theft and admitted to being in breach of an earlier sentence of six months imprisonment suspended for two years. The judge told him that he had been convicted on clear evidence, adding 'I am sure the jury was right'.

Three months later his appeal was lodged and Donald was released pending its adjudication. On his behalf it was urged that the judge was wrong to rule that it was impracticable to arrange a group identification; that he was wrong to allow the prosecution to ask Anne if she thought that the second robber had been on the parade, considering that she had not made a positive identification; that the identification by Pauline was unsafe because she had not described him in sufficient detail or heard his voice; and that there were further unsatisfactory features of a less substantial kind. The Court of Appeal adopted several of these arguments. They did not criticize the Judge's summing up of the identification evidence (which, it may be thought, was the central question) but allowed the appeal because they considered that the police did not do enough to set up a group identification. They regarded an identification at a confrontation as of little more value than a dock identification in court, and therefore as something to which little weight could be given.

This judgement (which has not featured in the published reports of the Court of Appeal) is of some importance because the Home Office circular is to be replaced by a code authorized by the Police and Criminal Evidence Act, 1984. That code is, at the time of writing, in its fifth draft. It enables the suspect to refuse to consent to a parade or a group identification but not to a confrontation. If the police cannot force a suspect to take part in a group identification, and if the judges regard a confrontation as being of very little value, then it will be made much more difficult for the police to obtain admissible evidence identifying persons who have taken part in serious arrestable offences. Problems will be all the greater when it is difficult to persuade members of the public of an appearance similar to the suspect to take part. The whole tendency is to place excessive emphasis upon the observance of formal rules concerning admissibility, when it would be better if, as the Royal Commission on Criminal Procedure (see paras 4.131-33) believed, evidence about identification, like evidence about confessions, were in each case evaluated on its own merits by the jury after instruction from the judge as to the way they should assess its reliability.

ADMISSIONS

One of the most difficult issues concerns the interviewing of suspects in custody. The police have been accustomed to interview those suspected of robbery and other offences by explaining to them the grounds for suspicion and asking them to account for those actions of theirs which have caused the suspicion. The preparation of cases for trial depends to a substantial extent upon the taking of suspects' statements so that the issues can be narrowed and the very expensive procedure of trial can focus upon the crucial contested elements. In an observational study conducted in four police stations for the Royal Commission, a Home Office research team found that of a sample of 187 suspects interviewed at a station 48 per cent made a full confession and 13 per cent an admission incriminating themselves to a lesser extent. Of 31 suspects who were not interviewed at the station, 12 had admitted the offence before they arrived there. The 187 interviewed at the station fell into two categories of equal size; of those with no previous criminal record, 76 per cent made a confession or admission while only 59 per cent of those with such a record did likewise. The difference was statistically significant. The importance of interviewing to the detection of crime is further increased by the information that of all detected crimes in England and Wales in 1978, no less than 25 per cent were detected as a result of admissions made by suspects and then taken into consideration when they were sentenced (Softley 1980, pp. 39–42).

There is reason to believe that the more experienced criminals, and those who have committed the more serious offences, are less likely to answer questions put to them by the police. There is also reason to believe that, partly because of the increased availability of criminal legal aid and of suspects' greater awareness of their rights, the proportion of suspects unwilling to answer questions is increasing; this reduces the ability of the police to detect crimes. It has therefore been argued that the power of the police to hold suspects in custody and question them before they have been able to instruct a solicitor should not be diminished.

For a statement to be admissible at trial, it must be made voluntarily, that is, without fear of prejudice or hope of advantage. The Royal Commission (para 4.73) concluded that the circumstances of questioning in modern police stations were so different in psychological terms from the kinds of conversation to which people are accustomed, that they were bound to press upon suspects' minds and cause them to speak when otherwise they would have stayed silent. Suspects sometimes made admissions to bring to an end a stressful situation or in the hope of being given bail (whether or not the police had said anything to suggest this). Some confessed in the hope of a lesser sentence, but sometimes, perhaps because of excessive pressure from the police, a suspect admitted to an offence which he or she had not committed. The suspect's rights have also to be protected. Since it is impracticable to divide suspects up into categories, providing strong protections for unintelligent, weak-willed and susceptible people, and different ones for those who have previous criminal records, it is inevitable that protections necessary for the former will also benefit less deserving people who are reasonably suspected of serious crimes. Criminal procedure in England and Wales is based on the principle that it is for the accuser to prove that the accused is guilty of a specific offence. The accused is under no obligation to respond to an accusation (though it may be contrary to his interests to exercise this right to the full). In police eyes this can become an obstacle that prevents their discovering the truth about events. In protecting the rights of the accused, the law weakens the security of the victims of crime and those who may become the victims of the unpunished offender. Experience in United States cities shows that as crime and the fear of crime increase, members of the public seek to defend themselves and refrain from exposing themselves to the circumstances in which they believe the risks to be greatest. They do not come together in revolt, demanding radical changes that will reduce the incidence of crime (and if they did those changes would entail a reduction in their own liberties).

The massive increase in robbery recorded in Tables 1 and 2 is likely to continue. It is notable that over half the robberies committed in Bristol in 1983 occurred in a relatively small inner city area. Perhaps the future will see the extension of the inner city pattern to the suburbs, with robberies becoming more widespread. The only genuine safeguard against such a development lies with the public and not with the police. It is members of the public who have to appreciate how many of the benefits of modern living create opportunities for crime. If crimes are to be prevented - and detection is one of the most important means of prevention - the public will have to take a more active part. The key to the detection of robbery lies in the information given to the police by members of the public and not in any reinforcement of police powers to question suspects in custody. Nothing indicates the nature of the problem better than the way the word 'informer' has been given an unpleasant savour. The member of the public who informs on a suspect performs a public service and should be praised for doing so. It is inevitable that some informers will be actuated by base motives but that should not be permitted to cloud the issue.

THE MANAGEMENT OF INVESTIGATIONS

Over the last twenty years there has been growing concern about the allocation of police resources. Police time has become more expensive and demands upon it have increased. This has provoked such questions as: How many policemen should there be? What proportion should be assigned to detective work? How should work be divided between detectives and patrol officers? Are detectives working efficiently? Are police resources being concentrated upon the most important tasks? How is the relative importance of different police tasks to be assessed? Answers to all these questions depend upon the development of effective measures. Police administrators have traditionally relied upon very crude measures; they have started out with ideas based upon the practices familiar to them, have relied upon their subjective assessments of priorities, and have responded to the views of politicians and others whom they have taken as representatives of public opinion. They could do little else.

Attempts have been made, most notably in the United States, to provide something better. Substantial research studies have been carried through, but their findings have been equivocal. The year-long controlled experiment involving motorized patrol in Kansas City seemed to indicate that patrolling by police officers in cars did little if anything to prevent crime. The big RAND Corporation study of The Criminal Investigation Process found that about 30 per cent of all arrests for crimes covered by the FBI index were effected by patrol officers responding to the scene of a crime. In roughly another 50 per cent of all index arrests, the identity of the offender was supplied by a victim or witness at the time of the initial crime report, leaving only about 20 per cent of arrests which could possibly be attributed to the efforts of investigative units. Most of these were eventually solved by subsequent patrol arrests, spontaneous information provided by members of the general public (as opposed to informants) or routine clerical actions such as the checking of automobile license plates. Only about 3 per cent of all index arrests appeared to result from special investigative efforts where organization, training or skill could make any conceivable difference (Greenwood 1980, p. 36).

A major study of the investigation of burglary and robbery in three United States cities was conducted over an eight month period during 1980 (Eck 1983). Between them, the cities produced a total of 323 robbery cases for analysis. For each one forms were completed recording the amount of time patrol and detective officers devoted to different kinds of activity while investigating the case. This produced a mass of quantitative data which was subjected to sophisticated statistical analysis, but it followed the cases only up to the point of arrest and the research (like much police research in the United States) was silent about the effect of court proceedings upon the attitudes and conduct of the police officers.   When the research worker tried to identify the kinds of police activity that had most frequently led to an arrest, he found considerable variation between the three police departments.   The only clearly consistent pattern was that interviews of informants (not of witnesses) by detectives was most likely to lead to an arrest.   One snag with this, of course, is that many robberies are committed out of public view.   There was some reason to believe that detection rates could have been improved had police officers spent more time exchanging information with colleagues, checking departmental records and interviewing informants.   The conclusions drawn from the research did not, however, contribute much to any answer to the difficult questions of resource allocation and management.   They indicated that the actions of both patrol and detective officers contributed to the solving of cases and that they had to complement each other.   Detectives had to be allowed flexibility, while their supervisors needed to be well informed about the individual skills of their detectives and the main features of the cases on which they were working.

The circumstances under which robbery investigations were carried out in central Bristol differ in many ways from those of the three United States cities just mentioned.   Possibly the main difference is that most of the Bristol offences were committed in an urban village in which a relatively high proportion of residents were known to one another and many people moved around on foot rather than in motor cars. Nevertheless, United States cities vary greatly and there are neighbourhoods which have some of the same features as St. Paul's.

Table 22
Methods of detection

	Victim	Witness	Informer	Surrender	Admission	Patrol	Investigation
Street Robberies	6	1	2	–	3	–	3
Shops and Houses	4	1	2	1	–	2	5
Other Robberies	5	–	–	1	1	–	5

Forty-two of the Bristol cases were detected. Table 22 compares the main factors which led to their being cleared up. The first column lists the cases in which the victim provided information which led to detection; sometimes he or she did so at the time the offence was reported but in one case it was not until nearly three months later that the victim happened to recognize the suspect. Sometimes the victim was able to make an identification only when helped, as in the case when he was shown photographs and then identified the suspects when confronted with the young men whose photographs he had singled out. The second column lists cases in which a witness other than the victim provided crucial information, while the third includes the cases in which an informer did likewise. In two cases the offender surrendered voluntarily. In four cases an offender admitted to the offence while being interviewed in connection with some other matter. After a bank robbery the offenders were apprehended as a result of a chase by patrol officers. In the remaining cases detection was achieved as a result of detective investigators obtaining information, comparing notes, questioning suspects, and so on, but elements of detective work entered into many of the detections listed in other columns also. For example, even in the two instances in which the offenders surrendered voluntarily, they did so because they had previous acquaintance with the police and knew what to expect. In one case an offender was willing to come and make an admission only to a particular detective whom he had known over several years. Any analysis which separates out these varying methods of detection must therefore be used with care. It does not provide findings of a character firm enough to sustain any definite conclusions about the best way to allocate detective resources. Nor does it seem worthwhile subjecting the data about the number of hours spent on different activities in the course of investigation to any more comprehensive analysis than the use which has been made of them in Chapters Two to Four.

Any attempt, by research, to collect information designed to improve the management of investigations, needs to start from a detailed study of present working practices, which include an extensive set of tacit understandings built up over the years. The key question is then whether any of these practices can be modified in a way that will improve output (for example a recent study by Tarling and Burrows (1984) found that in some other forces detectives spent between one quarter and one third of their time writing reports, and that there was scope to reduce the proportion of their time spent in this way). Responsibility for working practices must lie with the supervisors, though their power to modify them may be limited because, for good reason, so much authority has been delegated to detectives. It is difficult to envisage any way of testing what can be expected from the modification of existing practices other than that of controlled experiment. This would require (a) the selection of some measure of output, such as detection rates for a particular set of offences; (b) identification of all relevant variables affecting that which is to be measured; (c) identification of practices to be modified; (d) selection of one or more police units suitable for experimental change, matched with comparable units in which the practices are to be held constant; and then (e) modification of the selected practices in the experimental units for a period long enough to measure the resulting effects.

It is doubtful whether the conditions are present for a properly controlled experiment of the management of criminal investigations in the British police. The obstacles that would have to be overcome can be grouped in three categories; (i) detective work is subject to many contingencies. No one can predict when major crimes will occur or when there will be a sudden call upon the available resources. (The best time for anyone to commit a robbery in Bristol is when a major murder enquiry is underway!) When no such enquiries are in progress it may be possible to give careful attention to a crime report that at any other times might be given a low priority. The use of detective time has always to be assessed relative to the work on which the detective would otherwise be engaged, and that must vary. The CID is organized so that at times when, say, a sergeant is on leave, away attending a course, off sick, or engaged with a long trial, some detective constable is acting sergeant in his place. Continuous cover has to be provided, but contingencies such as these affect the resources available at any particular time. (ii) The delegation of authority has many positive features, not least that of maintaining high motivation, but it means that working practices are shaped to suit the personalities of particular individuals. Normally a uniformed officer takes a report of an alleged crime or makes an arrest. Whether or not he hands the matter over to a detective depends upon many factors, such as the seriousness of the offence, but one of them may be whether he is coming to the end of his shift. Whether the constable in question is keen or experienced may make a difference, as may the current detective workload. How the supervision of the investigation is carried out depends upon whether a detective takes over responsibility. If so, the Detective Inspector will allocate the case either to him or some other detective. The more serious the case, the higher the rank of the detective who takes charge. When the responsibility is left to a single detective, supervision is on a conversational basis with the detective reporting orally; after three months, if the case remains undetected, a written report is submitted to the Superintendant commanding the sub-division. Thus, as can be seen, working practices are so flexible and in places so informal, that it is difficult to introduce any experimental change. (iii) It is also difficult to agree upon a satisfactory measure of output or performance. No objective measure is likely to be acceptable. It would have to be complemented by subjective appreciations of relevant circumstances and this would probably make it impossible to decide whether the experimental change had any definite effects.

A negative conclusion like this also has its positive aspect, for it does not point to any possible weakness in the current management of investigations. The police cannot then be criticized for failing to take advantage of techniques that could improve their performance. At the same time, though, police administrators are left in a difficult position because they cannot be confident that their use of resources is correct. It might seem to the reader as if the information presented in the case histories summarized in Chapters Two to Four should be fairly readily available from police records. This is far from the case. The information was scattered and had to be assembled from a variety of sources, often from questions addressed to the detectives who had handled the cases. So much information comes to the police that it is a major task to determine what is important, what should be preserved and how access to it should be possible. There has to be a clear sense of the purpose for which records are being kept. Since the police are primarily concerned with what happens up to the stage when the prosecutor takes over, information which is not crucial to the prosecution may be neglected. Thus in the division where the research was carried out the Detective Superintendant found from checks upon case papers as they came back from courts that some additional charges (including further offences admitted and taken into consideration when the offenders were sentenced) had not been counted in the official statistics. When allowance was made for these the detection rate was improved by three per cent. From interviews with convicted house-breakers in prison, conducted on the undertaking that they would not be further prosecuted for confessions to other similar offences, the detection rate for burglary could be improved by 60 per cent. This suggested to him that the right men had been arrested but that the difficulty was of obtaining sufficient evidence to prosecute them for all their crimes.

The classification used in this report is not one that has been previously employed. This way of analyzing an offence and the methods of detection, could perhaps be used in other circumstances and give police officers a better understanding of the general picture. They can at times feel that they are in a situation in which they cannot see the wood for the trees, and the occasional analysis of a particular crime problem could help consideration of overall strategies. Certainly the question of information relevant to the management of investigations is one that will be of increased importance. The keeping of all records about investigation will no doubt soon be mechanized (and not just those pieces of evidence needed for the very biggest enquiries). This will bring into focus the problem of deciding just what information should be retained, how the data are to be protected and how the rights of individuals to privacy are to be safeguarded. The detailed consideration of what is entailed in investigation of a particular offence, like that of robbery, can provide the kind of evidence upon which any such debates need to be based.

Bibliography

BURROWS, John and Tarling, Roger, (1982), Clearing Up Crime, Home Office Research Study, 73, HMSO, London.

Crime Statistics for the Metropolitan Police District Analyzed by Ethnic Group, 1977-83, Home Office Statistical Bulletin 22/84, London, 1984.

ECK, John E, (1983), Solving Crimes: The Investigation of Burglary and Robbery, Police Executive Research Forum, Washington.

GREENBERG, BERNARD, et. al., (1975), Felony Investigation Decision Model - An Analysis of Investigative Elements of Information, Stanford Research Institute, Menlo Park, CA.

GREENWOOD, Peter W., (1980), The Rand Study of Criminal Investigation: the findings and its impact to date, pp 35-43 in Clarke, R.V.G. and Hough, J.M., (eds.), The Effectiveness of Policing, Gower, Farnborough.

HOUGH, Mike, and Mayhew, Pat, (1983), The British Crime Survey: first report, Home Office Research Study, 76, HMSO, London.

MAXFIELD, Michael G., (1984), Fear of Crime in England and Wales, Home Office Research Study, 78, HMSO, London.

SOFTLEY, Paul, (1980), Police Interrogations: an observational study in four police stations, Home Office Research Study, 61, HMSO, London. A slightly shorter version of this report was published in the same year as Royal Commission on Criminal Procedure Research Study, 4.

ROYAL COMMISSION ON CRIMINAL PROCEDURE, (1981), Report, HMSO, London.

STEER, David, (1980), Uncovering Crime: The Police Role, Royal Commission on Criminal Procedure Research Study, 7, HMSO, London.

TARLING, Roger and Burrows, John, (1984), 'The Work of Detectives', Policing, Vol 1, pp. 57-62.

Appendices

Appendices

Appendix 1

Reported Robberies

Any police officer taking a complaint of robbery should at the earliest opportunity complete the relevant setions of part A and submit it with form one. The investigating officer is responsible for the completion of parts A and B. When there is more than one suspect a part B should be completed for each suspect.

Date of Offence: Divisional Crime No:

Details of Complainant:

PART A TIME SPENT ON ENQUIRIES
(Estimated times must be as accurate as possible)

	UNIFORM		C.I.D. & SPECIALS (FCS, ETC.)	
	Constables	Others	Constables	Others
With Complainant inlcuding statement				
House to House				
S.O.C. Examination (including forensic)				
Tour area with Complainant				
At Hospital				
Showing Photographs				
Photofit				
Time with Eye Witnesses				
Observations at scene/in area				
Other Force Enquiries				
Dealers/Property Disposal				

Reported Robberies

Part B   SUSPECTS/CULPRITS ARRESTED OR INTERVIEWED

Arrest of Suspects

Investigation of suspect
(Background/movements)

Interviewing suspect

Identification Parade

Preparation of Case Papers

Court:-   Remands

                 Committal

                 Trial

Appendix 3

Reported Robberies

PART C   DETECTIVE INSPECTOR'S EVALUATION OF REPORT

Score

Offender

    Identifiable?
        (Yes – 5; Partly – 2; No – 0)

    Known?
        (Known – 5; Known and Named – 10)

    Places suspect frequents
        (If named – 10)

Movement Description

    On foot?
        (Score 1)

    Vehicle?
        (Vehicle only – 1; colour described – 2;
        make – 4; registration number – 8)

Physical Evidence

    Fingerprints
        (Score 5)

    Forensic
        (at scene, or clothing – 1)

Seriousness

    Injury
        (None – 1; slight – 2; serious – 8)

    Weapon
        (Knife – 3; gun – 10; other – 2)

    Offence occasioning public concern
        (score 5; if apparently by
        professional criminals – 10)

TOTAL

Appendix 4

Stanford Research Institute
Robbery Investigation Screening Model

INFORMATION ELEMENT	WEIGHTING FACTOR
Suspect Named	10
Suspect Known	10
Suspect Previously Seen	10
Evidence technician	10
Places Suspect Frequented Named	10
Offender Movement Description:	
On Foot	0
Vehicle (not auto)	0.8
Auto	1.5
Auto Colour Given	1.5
Auto Description Given	2.3
Auto License Given	3.8
Physical Evidence:	
Each Item	1.3
Weapon Used	1.8
Vehicle Registration:	
Query Information Available	1.1
Vehicle Stolen	2.3
Useful Information Returned	3.4
Vehicle Registered to Suspect	4.6

Rule: Circle the above weighting factors that appear in the incident report. If the sum of the factors of 10 or above, follow-up the case; otherwise suspend it.

Source: Greenberg et.al. (1975)

Index of cases